Exploring Music

Beth Landis

Buryl A. Red, arranger and consultant

HOLT, RINEHART AND WINSTON   New York, Toronto, London, Sydney

ISBN: 0-03-089540-5

9   039   9

Musical autography by Maxwell Weaner

Certain portions of the text appeared in *Exploring Music, The Junior
Book,* copyright © 1968 by Holt, Rinehart and Winston, Inc.

Picture Sources

p. iv—Elliott Landy for Magnum; Hugh Rogers from Monkmeyer; William Katz; William Katz; Douglas Jones from Look Magazine; p. 7—Erwin Kramer from
Photo Researchers; Winston Sutter from Photo Researchers; p. 15—Rhythm Band Incorporated, Fort Worth, Texas; M. Hohner, Inc.; p. 20—UPI; Irving Schild from
DPI; RCA; Jack Mitchell; Jackie Alper from DPI; RCA; Emil Schulthess from Black Star; United Artists; David Gahr; UPI; p. 23—Columbia Records; p. 25—French
Government Tourist Office; p. 26—Chinese Information Service; p. 27—Ken Kay from DPI; p. 29—Sidney Bernstein from Photo Researchers; p. 30—Horn-Griner;
p. 44—Wide World Photos; p. 50—Columbia Records; p. 53—RCA; p. 56—Gress-Miles Organ Company, Princeton; p. 57—Russ Kinne from Photo Researchers;
p. 61—"Haddam" from the "Musical Primer," Courtesy William M. Clements Library, The University of Michigan; p. 63—Source Magazine, Sacramento, California;
A graphically notated sketch of "Fragment" (1964), a composition for electronic sounds by University of Michigan School of Music Professor George Balch Wilson;
p. 66—Jean-Pierre Leloir; p. 77—Buddah Records; p. 81—Jazzmobile; p. 84—Harry Redl from Black Star; p. 92—Claus and Liselotte Hansmann; p. 93—Jerry Frank
from DPI; p. 94—Sigrid Owen from DPI; p. 108—Elliott Landy for Magnum; Buddah Records; United Nations; Culver Pictures; Lawrence Shustack from DPI; David
Gahr; Sybil Shackman from Monkmeyer; p. 120—permission: The Guthrie Children's Trust Fund. Photo by Robin Carson; p. 121—Vanguard; p. 125—Suzanne Szasz;
p. 128—The Bettmann Archive; p. 129—Courtesy, Oxford University Press, Mrs. Henry Cowell; p. 136—Roy Lindstrom from High Fidelity Magazine; p. 138—C. A.
Peterson from Rapho-Guillumette; UNESCO/Cart; Frederick Ayer from Photo Researchers; UPI; UPI; Helene Fischer from Black Star; p. 140—Marc and Evelyne
Bernheim from Rapho-Guillumette; p. 143—Viltis Magazine; p. 144—Fritz Henle from Photo Researchers; p. 145—George Holton from Photo Researchers; p. 152—
Teodulo Naranjo of Aguililla, Michoacan, Mexico. Photo by Arturo Macias; p. 153—Carl Frank from Photo Researchers; p. 157—Grant Heilman from Monkmeyer;
p. 159—Courtesy The Lynn Farnol Group; p. 171—Sony Corporation of America; p. 173—Roy Lindstrom from High Fidelity Magazine; p. 174—Roy Lindstrom from
High Fidelity Magazine; p. 175—Electronic music studio of the University of Michigan School of Music; p. 176-177—Serge Lido; p. 178—Jack Mitchell; p. 179—
Martha Swope; p. 180—Jack Mitchell; Ken Kay from DPI; Martha Swope; p. 181—Novosti from Sovfoto; Jules Zalon from DPI; p. 182—H. H. Kreider from Black
Star; Marc and Evelyne Bernheim from Rapho-Guillumette; p. 183—Alfredo Linares from Monkmeyer; Peter Larsen from Photo Researchers; p. 184—United Nations;
p. 185—Satyan from Black Star; Japan Air Lines; UNESCO/F. Pouey; p. 191—Bell Records; p. 194—Columbia Records.

Contents

Step Up Join In Sing Out! 1

Sing Out! 1; Let the Rafters Ring, 4; We'll Find
America, 7; The Tree of Peace, 11; Note Read-
ing for Boys Only, 13; Playing the Guitar, 14;
Instruments in the Classroom, 14; It's a New
Day, 16; It's a Small World, 18; Get Thy Bear-
ings, 19

The Music of Your Time, 21

Cloud—Chamber Music *(Partch)*, 23; When the
Bells Justle *(Foss)*, 24; Hyperprism *(Varèse)*,
24; Gargoyles *(Luening)*, 25; pai niao chao fêng,
26; Sonata No. 31 in G Major *(Cimarosa)*, 27;
Canzona *(Frescobaldi)*, 28; Violin Concerto in E
Minor, Opus 64 *(Mendelssohn)*, 28; Soldier's
Song *(Kodály)*, 29; Fantasia *(Mudarra)*, 29; Two-
Part Invention in D Minor *(Bach)*, 30; Sinfonia
(Berio), 31; This Is the Word, 31; The Content
of Music, 32

The Sound of Rock, 34

Spinning Wheel, 35; Day-Glo-Day, 38; The Beatles, 42; Eleanor Rigby, 42; When I'm Sixty-Four,
44

The Country Sound, 47

Green Green Grass of Home, 48; The Wreck of
the Old '97, 50; (Good Old Electric) Washing
Machine (circa. 1943), 51

Patterns and Designs in Music: Organization, 54

Patterns and Designs in Music: Theme and Variations, 55

Variations on "America" *(Ives)*, 56; Gymno-
pédie No. 1 *(Satie)*, 57; Two Variations on the
Theme *(Blood, Sweat and Tears)*, 57; Seven
Variations on God Save the King *(Beethoven)*, 58

Communicating Musical Ideas, 61

Experiments in Music I, 64

The Sound of Soul, 66

Wade in the Water, 66; Go Down Moses, 72; God's Goin' to Set This World on Fire, 74; An American Composer, 76; Scherzo (Humor) (Still), 76; O Happy Day, 77; I Wish I Knew How It Would Feel to Be Free, 80

Elements of Jazz, 82

It's About That Time (Davis), 84; Rhapsody in Blue (Gershwin), 84; Competition and Galop (Bernstein), 85; Ebony Concerto (Stravinsky), 85

Patterns and Designs in Music: Imitation, 86

Two-Part Invention in D Minor (Bach), 87; Symphony in B Flat for Concert Band (Hindemith), 88; Tallis' Canon, 89; Come, Quiet Hour, 90; Melody and Harmony, 90; Shalom, Chaverim, 91; Einundzwanzig, 91

Music of the Guitar, 92

Mounsier's Alamaine (Batchelar), 92; Prelude No. 2 in E Major (Villa-Lobos), 93; Alegria del Alosno, 93; Pantheistic Study for Guitar and Large Bird (Stuart), 93

Instruments of the Band and Orchestra, 94

Symphony for Band, Opus 69 (Persichetti), 95; Heroic Music (Telemann), 97; Kleine Kammermusik, Opus 24, No. 2 (Hindemith), 99; String Quartet in C Major, Opus 76, No. 3 (Haydn), 101; Gaucho Seranade (Bolognini), 101; Sounds from the Percussion Section, 103; Sketch for Percussion (Lo Presti), 103; Boléro (Ravel), 104; Symphony No. 4 in F Minor, Opus 36 (Tchaikovsky), 106

American Folk Songs Today and Yesterday, 109

Wayfarin' Stranger, 110; Wanderin', 115; Pastures of Plenty, 120; I'm Gonna Be A Country Girl Again, 121; He's Gone Away, 121; Whoopee Ti-Yi-Yo, 122; Joy Is Like the Rain, 125; The Power and Glory, 126

Charles Ives and his Music, 128

Fourth of July, 130; Sonata Number Four for Violin, 131; Memories, 132; The Circus Band, 134

Experiments in Music II, 136

Music from Distant Places, 139

Bwana, Ibariki Afrika, 139; Musical Instruments in Africa, 140; Sarakatsani Song, 141; Starlight Dance, 142; Nisiōtikōs Choros (Island Dance), 143, Landlord, 144

Sounds from the Far East, 145; Dhun, 145; Ketjak Chorus, 145; Echigoshi, 145

Scarborough Fair, 146; Henry Martin, 150; La madrugada, 151; El son del viento, 152; A la capotín, 152; Guantanamera, 154; Der Bergwalzer, 156; Songs of the Don Cossacks, 157

Patterns and Designs in Music: Ostinato, 158

Carmina Burana (Orff), 158

Broadway Musicals and Movie Music, 159

The Sound of Music, 159; Who Will Buy? 160; Shalom, 161; What's New Pussycat? 164

Experiments in Music III, 167

Patterns and Designs in Music: The Rondo, 168

Rondo for Bassoon and Orchestra (Weber), 169; Rondo (Cowell), 169; Swingin' Round, 170; Hey, Ho! Anybody Home? 170

Experiments in Music IV, 172

Dripsody (Le Caine), 171; Of Wood and Brass (Ussachevsky), 171

Sounds and Photo Study of Dance, 176

Dance of the Comedians (Smetana), 178; Navarraise (Massenet), 178; Infernal Dance of King Kastchei (Stravinsky), 179; Doudlebska Polka, 181

Your Career in Music, 186

More Songs to Sing, 188

Aquarius/Let the Sun Shine in, 188; Up and Get Us Gone, 192; Jenifer Juniper, 195; Hurdy Gurdy Man, 198; The Entertaining of a Shy Little Girl, 200; Green Fields, 203; All Lands and Peoples, 205; Summer Song, 206; Surfing Song, 207; O God, Our Help in Ages Past, 208; For Us a Child Is Born, 210; A Christmas Happening, 211

Revolutionary Ideas, Part I, 217

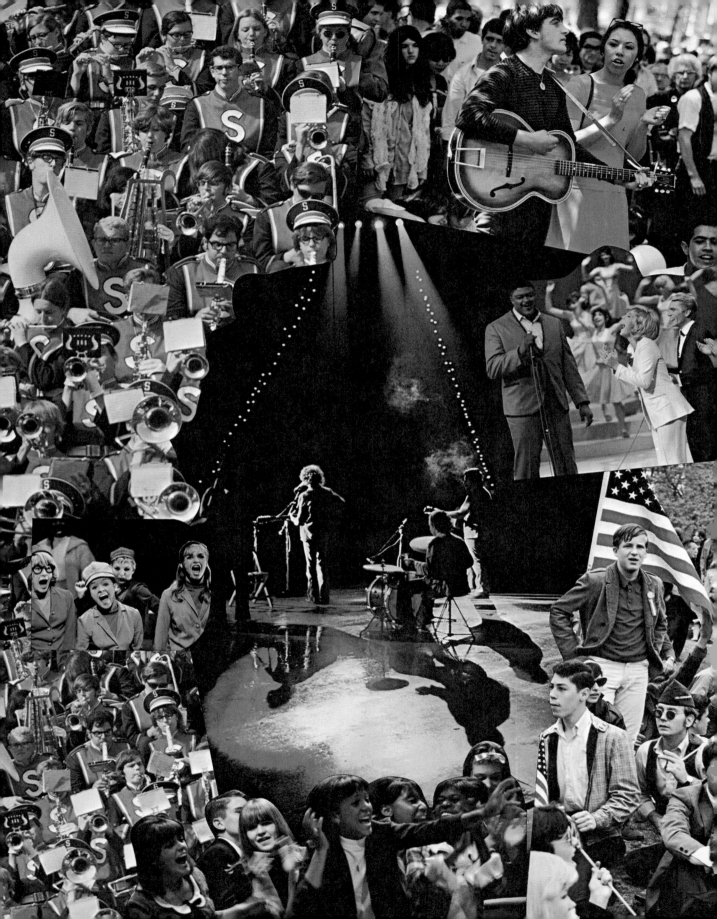

step up
join in
sing out!

Sing Out!

Words and Music
by Steve, Paul, and Ralph Colwell

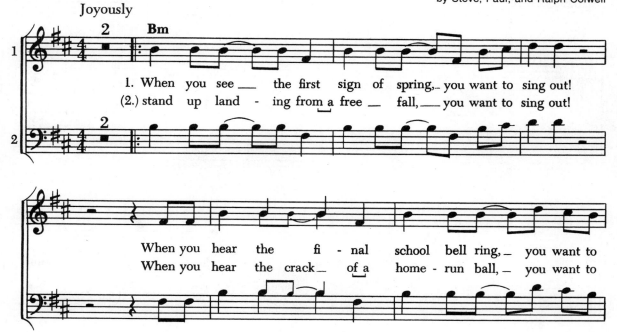

1. When you see __ the first sign of spring, __ you want to sing out!
(2.) stand up land - ing from a free __ fall, __ you want to sing out!

When you hear the fi - nal school bell ring, __ you want to
When you hear the crack __ of a home - run ball, __ you want to

sing out! You take off for the swim-min' hole _ with your
sing out! When you see the surf-er shoot the curl, _ from _

Ah, _____

faith-ful dog and your fish-in' pole, _ it seems that you can hear the whole world
out in space you _ view the world, _ it seems that you can hear the whole world

Ah, _____ Ah! _____

sing out! 2. Make a
sing out!

For some it's Tchai-kov-sky's Con-

cer-to; _____ for oth-ers it's rhy-thm and blues, _____

That sets off a feel-ing in-side of you, _ {and

Oo _____

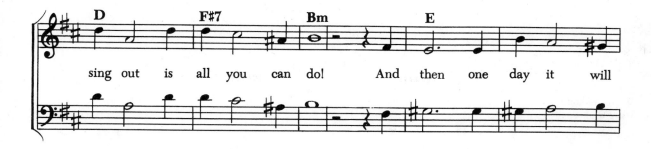

sing out is all you can do! And then one day it will

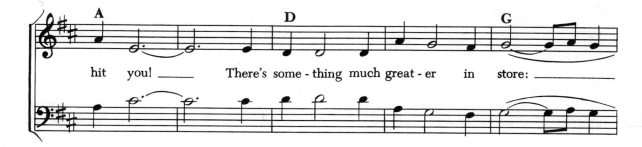

hit you! _____ There's some-thing much great-er in store: _____

_____ That we can do some-thing 'bout this old world, __ and

Oo _____

sing out like nev-er be-fore. Sing out!

Sing out! Sing out! _____

Let the Rafters Ring

Words and Music
by Dick Smith

5

show ev - ery - one that you care. ___ You got - ta

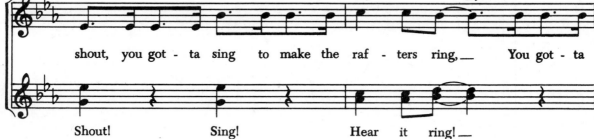

shout, you got - ta sing to make the raf - ters ring, ___ You got - ta

Shout! Sing! Hear it ring! ___

tell ev - ery - one ev - ery - where. ___ You got - ta

Tell ev - ery - one ev - ery - where.

shout, you got - ta sing to make the raf - ters ring, ___ You got - ta

Shout! Sing! Hear it ring! ___

show ev - ery-one that you care. ___ Let the raf - ters ring! ___

We'll Find America

Music by Sam Pottle
Words by Sam Pottle and
David Axlerod
Arr. B. A. R

9

The Tree of Peace

Music by Fred Bock
Words from "O Brother Man"
by John Greenleaf Whittier
Adapted by Fred Bock

Read the poem which is the basis for the text of this song, and discover its meanings. It was written by a famous American poet in 1848. The words in this new musical setting express contemporary ideals. They express ideals of generations of Americans who have sung them in various musical settings for more than a hundred years.

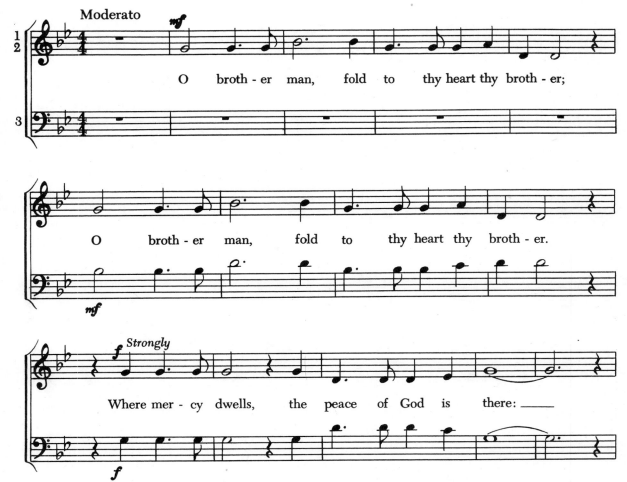

To live right-ly is to love one an-oth-er, Each smile a hymn, each kind-ly deed a prayer.

Then shall all the shack-les fall off and the storm-y clang-or of war's wild mu-sic o'er the earth shall cease! earth shall cease!

Love shall put out the burn-ing fire of an-ger,

And in its ash - es plant the tree of peace, And in its

ash - es plant the tree, plant the tree of peace! ___

Note Reading for Boys Only

Boys' voices are in several ranges and qualities which give richness and variety of timbre to the sound of class singing. To accommodate the various types of voices, notation of songs is somewhat different from the notation you were used to when everyone sang in a treble voice. The treble staff and bass staff both will be needed. (See grand staff on page 1.) One or two parts for boys may appear on the bass staff (as in "Tree of Peace" above). A part for boys may be written on the treble staff, and it may be sung in two ways. Sometimes the treble part is to be sung as notated, that is, it sounds at the pitch you would play on the piano when reading the notes. (See the song on page 4.) Sometimes it is to be sung an octave lower

than written, that is, it sounds at the pitch you would play on the piano if you play an octave lower than the notes are written. (See the song on page 38.)

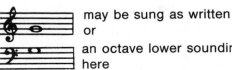

may be sung as written
or
an octave lower sounding here

Become fluent in reading the notation of your songs and producing the tone that is right for your voice and for the song arrangement. Change parts as your voice quality changes so that you can continue to sing comfortably.

Playing the Guitar

Playing the guitar is a popular musical activity in the United States. If you can play the instrument, or if you wish to learn, you can accompany many of the songs in your book.

The strings of the instrument are tuned from low to high — E, A, D, G, B, E — and cover a two-octave range.

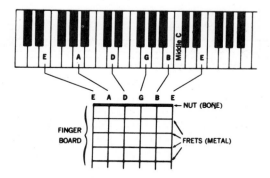

In the tablatures below, the numbers indicate the fingers of the left hand. A black circle indicates where the fingers should be placed on the strings. An open circle on a string indicates that you do not strum that particular string.

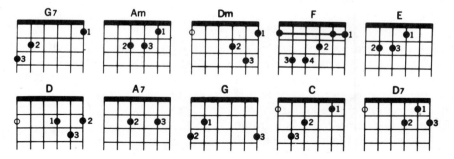

Instruments in the Classroom

Instruments will be very useful to you throughout your study of *Exploring Music, Book Seven*. Play the instruments you keep in your classroom, those you own individually, and those you can borrow from the band and orchestra or from other sources. You might purchase small, inexpensive instruments such as the recorder, harmonica, and melodica. If ten students buy recorders, and other groups of ten buy other instruments, you will be able to enrich your music-making with an interesting variety of sounds. Autoharps come in different sizes. Some of you may wish to purchase one to practice at home. In class, several autoharps can be played together for accompaniment. Bell sets and xylophones of different sizes, some with low tones, will be needed. Play any bass instruments that are appropriate such as string bass, bass guitar, or bass xylophone.

A variety of percussion instruments can be played for many musical purposes. Your activities will be more interesting if guitars are available. Some of you probably play the guitar already. Others may wish to develop skill on the instrument. Those of you who play band and orchestral instruments will find opportunities to play your instruments individually and in ensembles as you progress through your book. Pianists can contribute their skills. Sometimes you will be asked to invent new instruments. Whether you are developing a rock accompaniment, studying patterns of rhythm or melody in notation, or experimenting with original musical sounds, you often will find instruments to be the best medium for performance and creative exploration.

It's a New Day

Words and Music
by Bob Oldenburg

1. It's a new day,_ so come on,_ get
(2.) new day_ to chal-lenge_ the

New day! New day!

mov-in'. _____ It's a new day, get with it, start groov-in'. _____
young heart. _____ It's a new day, don't you want to take part? ____

___ Got-ta shoot for _ the moon, ride the _ bal-loon.
___ There are worlds yet _ to touch, stars yet _ to clutch.

There's a __ big job yet_ to do! Some-thing

Some-thing new,

It's a Small World

Words and Music
by Richard M. Sherman and Robert R. Sherman

You may have heard this song in the "Small World" exhibit at Disneyland. The writers are brothers who have composed many well-known musicals that young people enjoy, among which is "Mary Poppins."

This song has two melodies which can be sung together. The form of the song is ABA. Sing it in this manner:

  girls sing A alone
  boys sing B alone
  girls sing A$_1$ while boys sing B

Add this bell part, and play the chords on the autoharp as an accompaniment for the song.

A) It's a world of laugh - ter, a world of tears; it's a world of

A$_1$) There is just one moon and one gold - en sun, and a smile means

B) It's a small, a small world af - ter all, It's a

hopes and a world of fears. There's so much that we share that it's

friend - ship to ev - 'ry one. Though the moun - tains di - vide and the

small world af - ter all, It's a small world

time we're a - ware: It's a small world af - ter all. ____
o - ceans are wide, It's a small world af - ter all. ____

af - ter all, It's a small, small world. ____

Get Thy Bearings

Words and Music
by Donovan Leitch

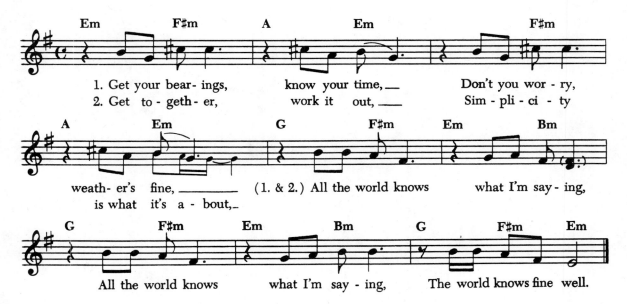

1. Get your bear- ings,   know your time, __   Don't you wor - ry,
2. Get to - geth - er,   work it   out, __   Sim - pli - ci - ty

weath- er's fine, _____ (1. & 2.) All the world knows   what I'm say- ing,
is what   it's a - bout, __

All the world knows   what I'm say - ing,   The world knows fine well.

The English singer Donovan (see photograph page 192) has said that pop songs are the literature of today with the words telling a story and the music making it fly or soar.

Listen to Donovan's performance of this song, and notice his folk-rock singing style. Notice the instrumental in which the saxophone improvisation and string bass are derived from jazz style. Listen to the song as recorded by a group of young people. Sing it in your own class singing style.

The following rhythm patterns may accompany this song. They can be played on guitar, bass, and percussion instruments.

the music
of your time

During your lifetime dramatic changes have taken place in the world of music. Electronic equipment has reached a height of development and common use. Almost all American homes have at least one television set. Recordings are purchased by the millions, especially by young people. People of your generation often hear the music of television, radio, and recordings several hours each day.

In this fast-moving age, popular music has become a fast-moving sound. A song can gain almost instant popularity because it is heard by millions of people at the same time. It forms a bond among those who like it as it is sung, played, and heard unceasingly. Since the song is a reflection of life at the moment, it often fades because other songs come to replace it. Electronic devices are a part of music-making equipment. Microphones, loud speakers, electronic organs and harpsichords, electrified guitars, and other instruments are important in the pop and folk music of today.

The electronic age has great effect on classical music, as well. Listeners nowadays are aware of composers' styles from early times to the present. Numerous performers and their specialties can be known whereas relatively few could be known through live concerts alone. The performer can study interpretation of many other performers while learning a composition.

Present-day technology and environment have important effects on the modern composer's creative efforts. Electronic music of many types is being composed by musicians who expect it to take a permanent place with other works of musical art. Composers today seek to expand the choices of musical sounds in many different ways. Some invent new instruments on which they can play sounds not available on traditional instruments. Others incorporate spoken words and noise sounds. Those who compose for traditional instruments and voices often use a basic twelve tones instead of eight. They create complex rhythms, melodies with wide range and unusual intervals, and harmonies of unlimited tones. This music too, is heard by great numbers of people through electronic media as well as in concerts.

In addition to music composed in the present and recent times, electronics have made it possible for us to know the music from practically all times and places. The drums of an African tribe, music from a village in India, fifteenth-century English madrigals, seventeenth-century Italian concertos, and nineteenth-century German symphonies all are familiar musical sounds today.

Most people enjoy many, if not all, types of music. Many perform rock, jazz, and classical music with equal interest. Most listeners collect records and attend concerts of several types and eras. As you extend your interests and skills, you will find unlimited musical sound available. There is keen excitement in the world of music, and through your own explorations you will share in this excitement.

today

with a few flicks of the FM dial

or by flipping a few discs on your own player

YOU CAN HEAR

A GREAT VARIETY OF THE WORLD'S MUSIC.

within an hour

you might hear

startling creations

of imaginative

american composers

of the

20TH CENTURY

Cloud-Chamber Music

by Harry Partch (1901-   )

Mr. Partch has spent a lifetime searching for ways to produce expressive sounds and to compose with these sounds. He wanted to have available forty-three tones to the octave, and he invented an instrument on such a plan. He wished to use the many inflections of the human voice and the sounds of spoken language. Many of his compositions include these sounds. Mr. Partch believes that a composer need not be limited to using sounds of the usual instruments, and he has built some very unusual instruments.

One of these, called cloud-chamber bowls, is made of a series of Pyrex carboys suspended on funnels tied with rope to a wooden frame. The bowls are played by tapping the edges with soft mallets, and a bell-like tone results. The tones are produced on ten or twelve sections of carboys.

In his composition, "Cloud-Chamber Music," Mr. Partch also used instruments which he calls adapted viola, adapted guitar, kithara I, diamond marimba, bass marimba, and California deer-hooves rattle, as well as human voices. Of special interest in this composition are the sounds of the new instruments, the use of gliding tones, and near the end, a Zuñi Indian motive. This is the first of several compositions in which this instrument is featured.

When the Bells Justle

from *Time Cycle*

by Lukas Foss (1922-   )

This composition was written in 1960 for soprano and orchestra. These words of the contemporary English poet A. E. Housman are sung:

> When the bells justle in the tower
> The hollow night amid,
> Then on my tongue the taste is sour
> Of all I ever did.

How is the mood of the poem expressed in the music? What sounds in the music imitate bell sounds? Compare the melody of the song with melody in traditional songs.

Hyperprism

by Edgar Varèse (1885-1964)

Edgar Varèse, though born in Paris, is called an American composer because he lived in the United States most of his life and did much of his work here. He was an important leader in the radical change of the standard concept of musical tone. Varèse was a man of the twentieth century with special interest in the activities and sounds of our time. He had a scientific and mathematical education as well as a musical one. He lived in noisy, big cities and believed in the expressive possibilities of noise sounds. He had the courage to replace traditional melody and harmony with other sounds, which he organized in new ways.

"Hyperprism" is composed for sixteen percussion instruments (played by several performers), seven brass, and two woodwind instruments. Identify the instrumental sounds and those not produced by the usual instruments. Notice the role of the groups of instruments.

"Baroque Experiment" by Fred Maddox. Oil on canvas 60" x 40" Grabowski Gallery, London, exhibited 1964

Gargoyles (Excerpt)

by Otto Luening (1900-   )

This is a composition for violin solo, which is played in the usual way, and electronic sound material which is produced on a machine called a synthesizer. For his synthetic sounds, the composer first prepares a complete program for every sound and silence of his composition. A computer, receiving the information, returns punched cards which can be fed into the synthesizer. The sounds the synthesizer produces may be imitations of traditional sounds or entirely new sounds. When the new sounds are recorded on tape, they can be used in various ways by the composer.

"Gargoyles" is composed of a subject and short variations. Compare your own thought and feeling responses to this music with your responses to a traditional composition. Explain why you do or do not like the composer's title.

...And Sounds from Far Away and Long Ago

pai niao chao fêng

(Hundred Birds Courting the Phoenix)

This is a North China folk song of the seventeenth century. In Imperial China (before 1912) it was played as banquet music by a large orchestra of Chinese instruments. On your recording it is played on the *nan-hu* and *cheng.* (In Chinese folklore the phoenix is queen of the birds.)

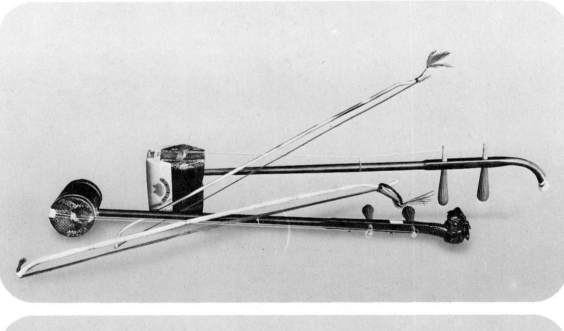

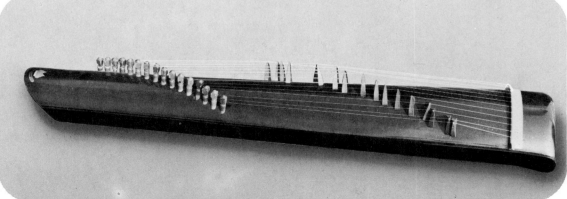

Sonata No. 31 in G Major

by Domenico Cimarosa (1749-1801)

This little sonata is played on a harpsichord. The harpsichord originated in the early fifteenth century when the hand-plucked instrument, the dulcimer or psaltery, was fitted with a mechanism. In the simplest form of the mechanism, each key controls a jack or plectrum that plucks rather than strikes (as in the piano) one string. In the sixteenth century, strings were added to each key, and stops achieved variation in tone color. Eventually the instrument had two manuals, six or eight stops, pedals (to enable changing stops without interrupting the playing), and five strings to a key. The instrument was replaced by the piano and rarely used in the music of the Romantic era. It is heard again nowadays in concerts, on recordings, radio, and in popular as well as classical music.

A sonata is written in a design that follows strict rules for introducing new material and for repeating and changing musical material. This one-movement sonata is a forerunner of the usual three- or four-movement form. The form in its full length is a very important one, used also in symphonies, concertos, and other types of compositions.

Canzona

from *Fiori musicali*

by Girolamo Frescobaldi (1583-1643, Italy)

On your recording the rendition of this "song" is by soprano, alto, tenor, and bass recorders. It is in two sections, one in $\frac{4}{4}$ meter and one in $\frac{3}{2}$. The melodic material of both sections is derived from the theme that follows.

...A Romantic Melody of the Nineteenth Century

Violin Concerto in E Minor, Opus 64

Second Movement

by Felix Mendelssohn (1809-1847)

The slow movement of Mendelssohn's violin concerto contains a beautiful lyric melody.

This main melody which begins with the notes below is heard in the first and third sections of the movement. The second section is built on another melody which grows to the climax of the movement. In the third section the main theme is given an altered accompaniment.

...AN old folk song ARRANGEd by A composer of the twentieth century

Soldier's Song

Hungarian Folk Song
Arranged by Zoltán Kodály (1882-1967)

The soldier sings "I am a soldier, defender of my country! But my mother weeps . . . O, my friends of the village, God's blessing on you. I am a soldier, defender of my country! But, my sweetheart, please wait for me. I am a soldier! My death knell has tolled, my sabre is polished . . . I will sacrifice my life for my country!"

...And a Composition Written for an Ancient Instrument but Performed on a Modern One

Fantasia

by Alonso Mudarra (1510-1580, Spain)

This music was composed during the sixteenth century for the vihuela, an early type of Spanish guitar, and has been transcribed for the modern guitar. The "free fantasy" was a popular form of composition for the instrument. From the music, what would you say the descriptive term and the title mean?

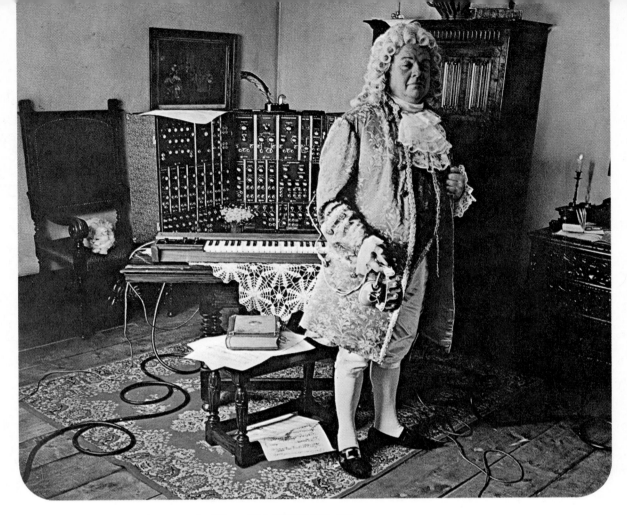

...OLD MUSIC
SOUNDING VERY NEW

Two-Part Invention in D Minor

by Johann Sebastian Bach (1685-1750)
played on the Moog Synthesizer

This "switched-on Bach" is played electronically on a Moog Synthesizer. Through two centuries the works of Bach have been transcribed by many persons for many different instruments. It seems natural that today they should be performed on the latest "instrument."

In the past fifteen years the synthesizer has been used increasingly to produce electronic music. In some ways it might be compared to an electronic organ with stops that imitate sounds of the violin, the flute, and so on. But the synthesizer is far more, for, through generators and modifiers, it has the ability to produce an infinite variety of sounds. Oscillators, filters, mixers, sequencers, and other units are mounted close together and interconnected. The performer (or often several people working together as performer) must choose from the array of sounds and effects.

The "Two-Part Invention in D Minor" was composed for the clavichord or harpsichord, the keyboard instruments of Bach's time. We are reminded of the sounds of these instruments in the new sound of the synthesizer.

...and MUSIC that hardly sounds like MUSIC, but IS

Sinfonia, Section Three

by Luciano Berio (1925-   , Italy)

Performed by symphony orchestra and a contemporary French group called the Swingle Singers, this composition gives us a strong impression of life today. How is this achieved? What sounds can you identify? Consider the composer's problem of writing down such a composition so that performers know what to sing or play; then consider the problems of the performers.

This Is the Word

by J. Marks and Performers
with words of Woody Guthrie

Some unusual music today is created with words. Six vocal soloists and a choir created this expressive sound with words of the folk singer Woody Guthrie. The words follow:

"I am trying to be a singer singing without a dictionary, and a poet not bound down with shelves of books . . . The word I want to say is easy to say, and yet is the hardest word I've tried to say . . . I will die as quick and as easy as I can to keep this one word living, because it keeps my whole race of people living, working, loving and growing on to know more and to feel more. This is the word I want to say."

The Content of Music

You have listened to musical sounds of many sources and in various combinations. As you consider the selections on the preceding pages, and others, you will find that they consist of elements and qualities that are common to all music. Whether the music has a rock beat, the drum beat of a primitive tribe, or the syncopation of jazz, the element of rhythm is basic to each. This element can be considered and analyzed in these and all other musics.

Whether the sounds are "natural" or "concrete," whether they are produced on newly-invented instruments, on folk or orchestral instruments, or by voices singing or speaking, tone color is a main quality of the sound. It is a quality of all music, from whatever source, and it can be observed in any music as can the elements and qualities referred to as pitch, texture, dynamics, and organization.

Each of the six categories of elements and qualities can be found in many simple and complex forms. A vocabulary of terms applies to each. The words help us to understand music and to communicate what we think about it. As you explore music in class and outside of class, let the common elements and qualities that are found in all music be the guide for your observations.

Pitch

horizontal (melody)
scale-wise
scale
major
minor
mode
pentatonic
diatonic
chromatic
motive
figure
pattern
phrase
range
vertical (harmony)
interval
quarter tone
chord
triad
cadence
modulation
key
key center

Rhythm

duration
beat
pulse
accent
pattern
meter
measure
syncopation
free rhythm
polyrhythm

Texture

thick
thin
chordal
homophonic
polyphonic
contrapuntal
bitonal
polytonal
chord stream
tone cluster

Listen again to excerpts or to entire compositions to further explore the musical content indicated. In your comments use terms listed on the chart.

1. Compare the pitch intervals and range of the folk melody, "Soldier's Song," page 29, with those in "When the Bells Justle," page 24.

2. Compare the melody of the seventeenth-century "Canzona," page 28, with the melody of the nineteenth-century *Violin Concerto in E Minor, Opus 64,* page 28. Compare the texture of the accompaniments.

3. Compare the sound sources, rhythm, melody, and texture of the ancient Chinese "pai niao chao fêng," page 26, with those of the contemporary "Cloud-Chamber Music," page 23.

4. Review "Hyperprism," page 24, and "Sonata No. 31 in G Major," page 27. Analyze the organization and dynamics of each.

5. Review "Fantasia," page 29, and "Two-Part Invention in D Minor," page 30. Comment on texture and organization of each.

6. Review "Gargoyles," page 25, "Sinfonia," page 31, and "This Is the Word," page 31. Analyze pitch content, texture, dynamics, and organization of each.

Dynamics

pianissimo (pp)
piano (p)
crescendo
mezzo forte
forte (f)
fortissimo (ff)
intense
climax
decrescendo

Sound Sources and Tone Color (Timbre)

natural
concrete
vocal
instrumental
string
woodwind
brass
percussion
skin
metal
glass
wood
bright
dark

Organization

form
design
unity—variety
tension—release
balance
order
theme
episodes
sectional
two-part
three-part
imitation
canon
theme and variations
repetition
sonata-allegro
rondo
coda

the sound of rock

In the mid 50's and 60's rock developed as a new musical expression of youth. For nearly twenty years it has dominated pop music, and some observers believe it will have a lasting influence. Rock began very close to grass roots traditions of the people. Rhythm and blues was a prominent influence in the styles of Elvis Presley and other early rock singers. Folk groups such as Peter, Paul and Mary sang old folk songs in a new way.

The Beatles helped make rock an international language by taking the native American idiom and creating a unique style that became popular everywhere. Today's rock has no stylistic limitations. Country and western, jazz, soul, Afro-Cuban, classical, and electronic music are the sounds heard in current rock.

Rhythm is the main musical material of rock style with its distinctive beat. The harmony at first was like folk harmony with the fundamental chords in prominence. More variety and more unusual harmonies are common now. Rock melodies often are in a small range and take the natural rhythm of the words. Other times rock melodies employ extreme ranges and unusual intervals. The lyrics of many early rock songs were from old folk songs, or they were "yeah's" and "ah's" and other sounds. Often singers improvised words as they performed. Lyrics have become more and more important. Bob Dylan, who came from the folk-song movement, became one of the most significant rock song writers. Many of his lyrics, along with those of some other writers, are considered to be significant poetry carrying important messages.

Electric amplification of instruments is a prominent part of rock sound. Guitars, bass instruments, organs, pianos, and even drums are amplified.

Recordings are the true medium for rock performances. Often a rock song is conceived in a studio for a specific recording. In this, rock is different from folk and jazz which always is centered in live performance. Live performance is nonetheless vital to rock. The West Coast was especially influential in setting trends in live performance with outdoor festivals and light shows. Rock groups have collaborated with symphony orchestras and other classical musicians in concert halls across the country. Audiences often listen in concert manner, or they dance, or combine the two in one evening. The influence of rock is apparent in movies, Broadway musicals, and pop art. The music called "rock" has made an enormous impact.

34

Spinning Wheel

Words and Music
by David C. Thomas
Arr. B. A. R.

you nev-er learn,—

Ride a paint-ed po-ny, let the

Spin-ning Wheel— turn. Did you find your di-rect-ing sign— on the

straight and nar-row high - way?— Would you mind— a re-

flect-ing sign?— Just let it shine— with-in your mind,— and

show you— the col-ors— that are real.—

Some-one is wait-ing just for you,— Spin-ning Wheel

spin-ning true,— Drop all your trou-bles by the riv-er - side,—

Catch a paint-ed po-ny on the Spin-ning Wheel— ride.

Develop your own rock accompaniment for "Spinning Wheel." The chord progression E7 A7 D7 G may be played throughout the song.

Traps may ad-lib with rim shots on beats 2 and 4.

Develop an introduction similar to that on the recording. Play the chord progression first on a bass, with the guitar, cowbell, tambourine, and drums, or instruments you substitute, coming in one at a time.

Develop a coda similar to that on the recording. Play the chord progression in $\frac{3}{4}$ meter, one chord to a measure. Play with a strong oom-pah-pah rhythm to suggest a carousel.

The recording of the song has been made with voices on the left channel, instruments on the right channel. By turning off the left channel of a stereo record player, you will hear the instrumental accompaniment only. This will be useful to you in several ways. You may practice your own accompaniment with the instruments on the record or with the voices. You can practice singing with the voices on the recording or with the accompaniment.

Day-Glo-Day

Music by Buryl Red
Words by Ragan Courtney

ping time,— It's a day-glo - day, —   It's a day - glo - day, _____

Hey! __   Bah, bah, bah, bah, bah, — bah, bah, bah, bah, bah!

Bah, bah, bah, bah, bah, — bah, bah, bah, bah,

Ev - ery-thing you see seems bound _ in a bub - ble, Ev - ery-thing you say seems pro-

found as a bub - ble. Ah, _____ ah, _____ It's a day - glo - day,—

__ Hey, hey, hey, hey, hey,   It's a day- glo - day,__ Hey, hey, hey, hey, hey,_

__ Hey! __   It's a day - glo - day,   It's a day- glo - day,

It's a day - glo - day, _____   Hey!

The suggested patterns below will help you begin your class rock accompaniment for "Day-Glo-Day." Play the instruments suggested or other instruments available to you. Improvise the remainder of the accompaniment as you go. There are two recordings on your record: first a complete version, then the rhythm section separately. You can practice your accompaniment with the rhythm recording, and the rest of the class can sing the voice parts.

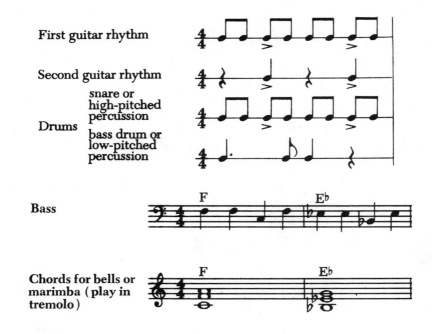

These parts may be played with the song on B flat trumpets or clarinets (the lower part is optional). Or you may write it in the key of F, and play it on flutes, bells, marimba, or other melody instruments.

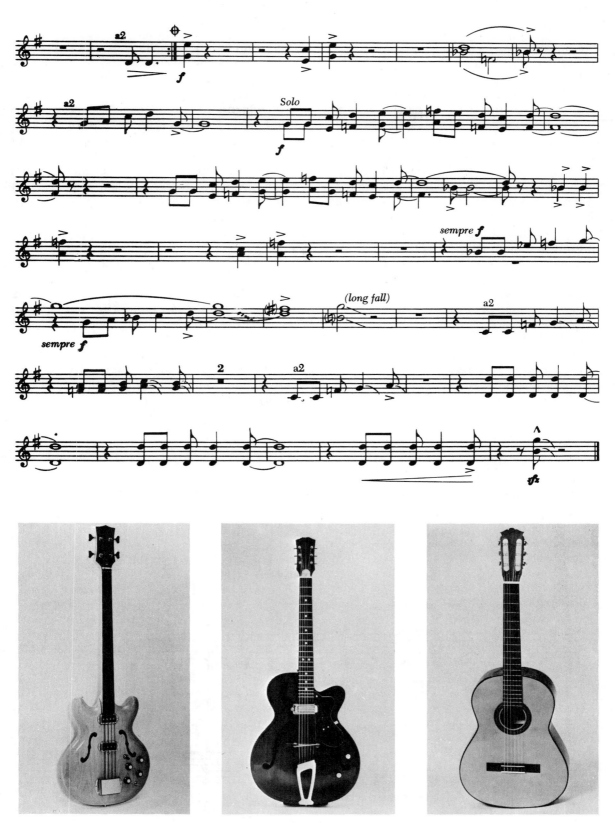

BASS GUITAR

ELECTRIC GUITAR

ACOUSTIC GUITAR

The Beatles

Some observers feel that the Beatles have had more influence on popular music than any composer-performers who have entered the field. The English group consisting of John Lennon, Paul McCartney, George Harrison, and Ringo Starr became popular in England in the early 1960's immediately following the great popularity there of Elvis Presley, the early rock performer from the United States. The Beatles developed a strong style and unusual authority in their music. With an air of carefree enthusiasm, fun, and happiness, their songs won audiences in the United States from the time of their first appearance here in 1964.

From their first great success, "I Want to Hold Your Hand," to the time when the quartet broke up in 1969, the Beatles recorded enormous numbers of songs and appeared before hundreds of live audiences and on television. They performed many variations of rock styles. Some of their songs were in rhythm and blues style, others in country and western, still others in folk and ballad styles. Some of their songs included foreign languages and reflected foreign cultures. George Harrison played the sitar which he learned from the Indian performer Ravi Shankar. Different eras of classical music such as the Baroque were imitated in some of the Beatles' music. The group explored contemporary electronic effects. Most of the words for the Beatles' songs were written by John Lennon and Paul McCartney, and these gave further distinction to the music of the quartet.

"Eleanor Rigby" is one of many songs that comment on life today. In their performance of the song the Beatles made interesting use of the classical string quartet for accompaniment. You will hear a similar accompaniment on your recording.

The Beatles' many styles included even the barbershop sound in "When I'm Sixty-Four." On your recording listen for tack piano, tuba, percussion, harmonica, and tenor banjo.

Eleanor Rigby

Words and Music
by John Lennon and
Paul McCartney

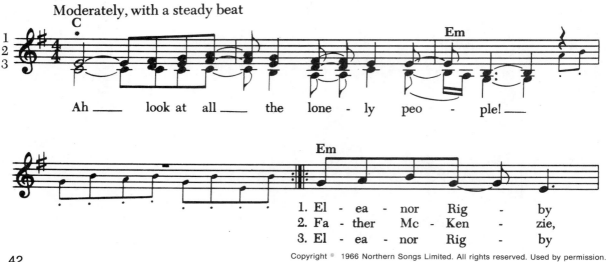

picks up the rice ___ in the church ___ where a wed - ding has been. ___
writ - ing the words ___ of a ser - mon that no - one will hear; ___
died in the church ___ and was bur - ied a - long ___ with her name; ___

C6   Em
___ lives in a dream, _____ Waits at the win - dow,
___ no - one comes near. _____ Look at him work - ing,
___ no - bod - y came. _____ Fa - ther Mc - Ken - zie,

wear - ing the face ___ that she keeps ___ in a jar ___ by the door. ___
darn - ing his socks ___ in the night ___ when there's no - bod - y there. ___
wip - ing the dirt ___ from his hands ___ as he walks ___ from the grave. ___

C6   Em   Em7
___ Who is it for? _____
___ What does he care? _____ } All the lone - ly peo-
___ No - one was saved. _____

Em6   C   Em
- ple, where do ___ they all _____ come from? ___

                                                              3rd time to Coda
Em7   Em6   C
All the lone - ly peo - ple, where do ___ they all ___ be - long? ___

1. Em   2. Em   D.C. al Coda   Coda Em

When I'm Sixty-Four

Words and Music
by John Lennon and
Paul McCartney
Arr. B. A. R.

As an introduction to the song, sing this melody on "doo" or play it on an instrument.

Play the chords on autoharp, ukelele, banjo, or guitar with strong accents on beats 2 and 4.

Old-fashioned tempo!

1. When I get old - er los - ing my hair, —
2. I could be hand - y mend - ing a fuse —
3. Send me a post - card, drop me a line —

the country sound

"Country" is a new term for an old music that has been part of the story of America since before the Revolutionary War. Beginning with ballads brought from England and changing them to fit the new life, colonists sang folk songs. In the mountains and back-country areas across the South to East Texas, singing overcame the loneliness of the frontier. Hillbilly folk songs of the rural South were the beginning of music we now call country music. Cowboy songs from Oklahoma, Texas, and Colorado became a part of the country literature. Sentimental religious songs, love ballads, songs of the West such as "Way Out West in Kansas" were heard on recordings and radio and expanded the popular music we call "country."

Family singers such as the Carter Family made millions of recordings in the 20's and 30's and were heard on popular radio programs. The giant of country music radio shows, Nashville's "Grand Ole Opry," began in 1926, reached the height of its popularity in 1939, and made fiddle music and hillbilly singing known everywhere. In the 30's when performing stars arose and began to vie for recognition, the folk aspect of country music became less important than the commercial. Newly written arrangements of old songs were pushing traditional versions aside. Meanwhile, the Library of Congress and various folklore societies were gathering together the original songs, and these form a large literature on records, tapes, and in books.

Country music passed through the phases of cowboy stars such as Roy Rogers, Gene Autry, the western swing bands of the dance halls, and the honky-tonk sound of the forties. Such names as Roy Acuff, Hank Williams, Tex Ritter, and Ernest Tubb are very familiar to lovers of country music. The music began to be referred to as "country" or "country-western" because some people thought "hillbilly" to be a degrading term. Country songs often were top hits on the pop lists, and the number of vocalists increased. When rock and roll emerged in the 50's, country music was influenced and sometimes modified toward the rock style. Modern country-pop of the 50's and 60's was largely a product of Nashville which became one of the largest recording centers. The "Nashville Sound" included background choruses, vocal groups, soloists, and professional instrumentalists. In bluegrass style there is no amplification of the five-string banjo and country fiddle. This style is much like the authentic old-time country music and was received as a fresh sound in American pop music. It has great appeal in concerts in the cities as well as elsewhere and on TV and recordings.

Today we hear country music that reflects each of the phases of its history. As in other music, many styles are a result of years of development. Country music which had its origins in early America continues to have vitality and to be a strong part of our folk-pop tradition.

Green Green Grass of Home

Words and Music
by Curly Putman
Arr. B. A. R.

1. The old home town looks the same, As I step down from the
(2.) old house is still stand-ing, Though the paint is cracked and

train, And there to meet me is my Ma-ma and Pa-pa.
dry, And there's that old oak tree that I used to play on.

Down the road I look, and there runs Mar-y, hair of gold and
Down the lane I walk with my sweet Mar-y, hair of gold and

lips like cher-ries: It's good to touch the green, green grass of
lips like cher-ries: It's good to touch the green, green grass of

Country music sometimes has elements of gospel style. This song is a good example. Notice, for instance, the "Amen" cadence at the end. Country music also has chromatic embellishment. Find examples in this arrangement. Here are some ideas for instrumental chromatic embellishment:

The recording is typical of the "Nashville Sound." Instruments such as the bass guitar and steel guitar are especially identified with this sound. Notice also the piano "fills" so typical of country music.

The Wreck of the Old 97

Performed by Lester Flatt and Earl Scruggs

This ballad relates the story of the wreck of the Southern Railway train between Monroe and Spencer, Virginia in 1903. The railway agent saw the wreck, and the words of the song came from his report. The tune was taken from an older song, "The Ship That Never Returned." The song was first recorded in 1923 after twenty years of being passed around by singing. No doubt it had been changed many times in those years. A Virginia hillbilly singer, Henry Whitter, had kept the ballad alive by singing it in his home area, and he recorded it first. This recording was one of the earliest commercial ventures in hillbilly music, and its popularity inspired many other singers to become performers of this type of music. This recording and those that soon followed made hillbilly music nationally prominent and started its great commercial success.

Lester Flatt grew up in a folk-singing family in Virginia and was singing for church and community gatherings at the age of seven. He is well known as a vocalist and guitarist. Earl Scruggs first heard the banjo played by his father. He developed his own banjo technique which dazzles listeners. His "three-finger" technique is a standard in bluegrass style. Scruggs is noted in the *Encyclopedia Brittanica* as the modern master of the banjo. Flatt and Scruggs have been popular recording and television performers.

(Good Old Electric) Washing Machine (circa. 1943)

Words and Music
by John Hartford

1. Well, I sure do miss that good old e-lec-tric wash-ing ma-chine, The one that we ain't got 'round here no more, And I sure do miss that big round tub and them stomp-ing, swing-ing sounds, And I miss them groov-y pud-dles on the floor.

2. Well, I cry when I see that brand new au-to-mat-ic wash-ing ma-chine, 'Cause I'm sen-ti-men-tal for the old ma-chine still yet, 'Cause the old one real-ly looked like a real live wash-ing ma-chine, But the new one just looks more like a tel-e-vi-sion set.

1. Create your own "down home" accompaniment. On a violin imitate the sound of a country fiddler by playing only on the open strings.

Play the chord symbols in the following manner:

for D chords play

for G7 chords play

for A7 chords play

Make up your own rhythm as you follow the chord symbols.

An introduction for the fiddle might be:

1. Well I

2. Tune four jugs to these notes:

Follow the chord symbols and play a bass line on the jugs:

for D chords play

for G7 chords play

for A7 chords play

3. Make a washtub bass (washtub, broomstick, and cord), and play the same bass line with the jugs.

4. If you have a harmonica in C, play the G7 chord in a "shuffling" rhythm each time it appears.

5. Other appropriate instruments are banjo, washboard, and squeeze horns in various pitches.

6. Improvise a piano accompaniment.

Listen to the recording. Some of these instruments play patterns similar to those above. Remember, in good "Nashville" style, you always "fill" (improvise) the "holes" (rests) in the melody.

John Hartford is a popular song writer and musician. Among the songs he has written is "Gentle on My Mind." He also wrote the poem that follows.

Earthwords

This white (record) jacket is really black
except for the white areas
acknowledging these words
and the black is really white
except for the black areas
that define the white . . .
the black and white so depend on each other
Sound cannot be sound
unless it is acknowledged by silence
the "is" and the "isn't"
so depend on each other
A soul doesn't really feel it is a soul
until some other soul
acknowledges awareness of its presence . . .
people so depend on each other
Escaping from indifference
and possessed of a basic natural showmanship
we each try to prove we exist
during our short journey to the grave . . .
searching for love and hate . . .
that we may confront them and hear them say
either "you is" or
"you ain't" . . . then at least we know
"we are"

patterns and designs in music: organization

Organization is one of the most important aspects of music. No matter how interesting individual musical ideas may be, they do not form a musical composition until they are organized. In order to gain an understanding of the possibilities of organization, complete some experiments. Develop ideas of design with written symbols. Then develop compositions in musical sound in the same designs.

Draw squares, circles, and triangles in a horizontal line in an arrangement you feel to be interesting. Start with a simple design with no symbols overlapping. Work alone using one or a few percussion instruments or any sound-makers you choose. Invent a rhythmic pattern to be represented by each symbol. Develop a complete composition represented by your written symbols.

In several experiments expand this idea in different ways. Use additional symbols in your written designs. Arrange them in different levels or lines. Let some overlap, others stand alone, and indicate variations of some. Use any mathematical or artistic principles you know to develop interesting designs.

Work with a few classmates to organize musical sounds represented by the symbols. Incorporate any sounds you believe to be musical. Play percussion, melody, or harmony instruments; use voices, electronic sounds, or environmental sounds in any way that results in interesting music. A written symbol may stand for a single rhythmic or melodic pattern, for a simple combination, or for a whole block of sound.

When you have compositions you like, practice until you can perform them well. Tape them, and then consider each one. Answer these questions in your considerations.

Are there enough sound elements to provide variety?
Are there too many elements with the result of a hodgepodge?
Are the elements sufficiently related to make a satisfying composition?
Is the organization clear, or does it seem confused?
Is familiar material (material already presented) boring when it is heard again, or does it continue to be interesting? Explain why.
Does the organization allow for development of some of the elements?
Does the composition have a clear beginning, climax, and closing?
Tell why you think listeners would or would not find it enjoyable and worthwhile to hear the composition more than once.

patterns and designs in music: theme and variations

In writing music, composers often state a musical idea and then repeat it. The repetition may be exact, or it may be changed or varied from the original. All compositions require some writing of variations. The composer may write a whole set of variations on a theme, or just one variation. Variations may be written for a theme, a phrase, or a few notes. In order to understand the variations principle, experiment with ways to vary musical patterns.

1. Play this rhythmic pattern on any percussion instrument.

Find several ways to vary the pattern by rearranging the notes, keeping the eighths and sixteenths together in their groups. Find several other ways to vary the pattern by changing some of the note values, retaining four beats in each measure. Write some of your variations. Play them from notation.

2. Play this pattern on any melody instrument.

Find several ways to vary the pattern by changing note values only. Change the pattern by substituting some notes of different pitches, but keep the same note values. Create a melodic variation by adding notes. Create a rhythmic variation by changing the meter to $\frac{5}{4}$, adding enough beats to complete four measures. Turn the melody into a march; into a waltz.

3. Harmonize one of the variations you created in assignment 2. Ask someone to sing your melody while you sing a harmony part composed "by ear." Or write the melody and harmony and ask a classmate to perform with you. Or sing the melody and play a harmony part on some instrument. Your harmony part might be a countermelody, or it may be a chordal harmony.

4. Create a variation on the melody by playing in the key of C minor. Change each E to E flat and each A to A flat.

5. Work with a few of your classmates and create short compositions using several percussion and melody instruments. Develop interesting variations. Be able to demonstrate the original melody and the variations to the rest of the class.

Variations on "America"

by Charles Ives (1874-1954, USA)

Ives wrote this composition when he was sixteen years old and played it in an organ concert in his church on the Fourth of July. He said that playing the last variation was "almost as much fun as playing baseball." The composition is full of humor which the young composer achieved by making good-natured fun of some of the commonest musical sounds he knew. The usual patterns played by church organists, the band music so popular at this time, and the polonaise rhythm used by Chopin and other composers were presented with tongue-in-cheek humor.

This may be his earliest work with polytonal harmony. In it we hear the beginnings of ideas that were developed throughout the life of the imaginative and talented composer. The composition consists of an introduction, the full hymn played as the theme, five variations, and a coda.

Introduction	Theme played in various keys with modulations commonly played by church organists, full organ sound, introduction in familiar ABA design.
Hymn Theme	Played straight.
Variation I	Theme once; patterns of thirds; scales; cadenzas played by right hand above theme played by left hand.
Variation II	Theme once; combined keys; shifting keys; "laughing" chords; barbershop cadence.
Polytonal Interlude	Abbreviated theme played in chord clusters in the right hand, imitated in a different key in the left hand beginning in second measure.
Variation III	Theme played twice with skipping rhythm of a nursery tune; second time new left hand part, funny cadences.

Variation IV	Theme once with second part repeated, minor key, polonaise rhythm:

$\frac{3}{4}$ ♪♫ ♫ ♫ ♪ ♫ |

Polytonal Interlude	Last and first phrases of theme combined within polytonal chords.
Variation V	Theme twice, imitating band music, pedal bass imitating bass horns below chordal theme; second time, pedal marching bass plus chordal theme plus ornamented third part in treble.
Coda	Fragments of theme built to fortissimo; chordal theme with ornamental countermelody to brilliant close.

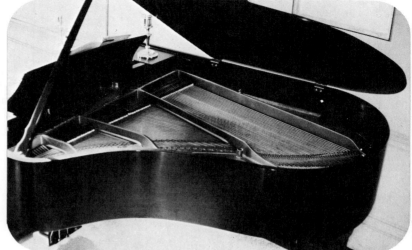

Gymnopédie No. 1

by Erik Satie (1866-1925, France)

Two Variations on the Theme

By Blood, Sweat and Tears

Listen to the composition in its original form. Listen to the two variations by Blood, Sweat and Tears. In the first variation what instruments replaced the piano? How much of the original melody and accompaniment was retained? What do you think to be the purpose of the ending of the variation?

In the second variation what instruments replace the piano? What of the original composition is retained? What is added?

This little composition by Satie has been transformed many times. Debussy arranged it for orchestra. Ravel imitated portions of it. Blood, Sweat and Tears gave us new versions of it. What do you think to be the qualities in the original that were so appealing?

By playing in another key, you can play the melody on your bells or other classroom instruments. Try making your own new version, playing on any instrument you choose.

Seven Variations on God Save the King

by Ludwig van Beethoven (1770-1827, Germany)

The Theme

Variation I Begins

Variation II Begins

Variation III Begins

Variation IV Begins

Variation V Begins

Variation VI Begins

Variation VII Begins

The Coda includes a six-measure **Adagio** section and the closing **Allegro** section, both in $\frac{3}{4}$ meter.

Listen to the composition on several occasions, and share comments on all that you heard. Later listen to each variation more than once, and discover answers for these questions.

1. How did Beethoven change the hymn tune in making it his theme?

2. In the first section of Variation I how did Beethoven change the melody line? In the second section why does the melody sound much like that of the theme?

3. In studying Variation II, find the notes of the melody in the measures on page 58. How do they compare in time value with the original notes?

4. What words can you think of to describe the sound of Variation III? How did Beethoven achieve the sound you described?

5. What is the character of Variation IV and of Variation V? Why do you think Beethoven developed the sharp contrast at this point?

6. In Variation VI which musical element is most changed from the original theme?

7. How is the sectional form of Variation VII different from the form of the theme?

8. In which of the variations did Beethoven stay most closely to the original theme? In which did he move farthest from it?

9. Compare the six basic elements and qualities (pages 32-33) of this composition with those of the Ives composition (see page 56).

10. Consider the styles of the two composers. What musical preferences of each can be heard in these compositions? What characteristics of the personality of each man and of the time in which he lived can you detect?

communicating
musical
ideas

Devising symbols for communicating music has been a problem for ages. The ancient Greeks and Romans had systems based on letters of the alphabet. In the tenth century Guido d'Arezzo took the syllables *ut, re, mi, fa, sol, la* from words of a Latin hymn and gave these names to the diatonic pitches c, d, e, f, g, a. The *sol-fa* method continues to be one of the methods used in reading music.

By the fourteenth century, church musicians had worked out a system of neums or signs which they used to notate songs of the church and of the minnesingers of the Middle Ages.

NEUMS:

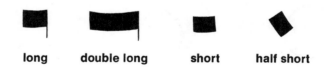

| long | double long | short | half short |

At first the neums could only indicate the general contour and approximate rhythm of a melody so that the singers could only identify songs already known to them. Later, as more shapes were added, it was possible for a singer to sing the approximate tones indicated by the shaped notes.

Song in Shape notation—music printed in America in 1803

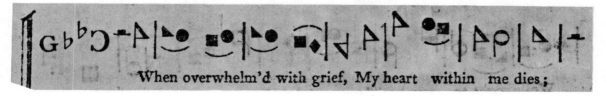

When overwhelm'd with grief, My heart within me dies;

When the staff was invented, more exact pitches could be indicated.

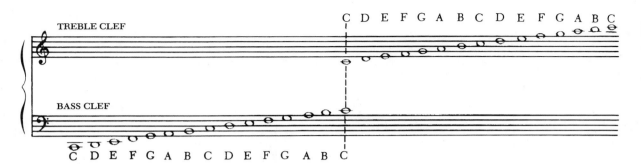

Today notes are recognized by their appearance and are identified by names referring to their relative time values.

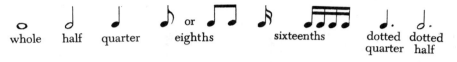

Clef signs first appeared in the neum system, and many such signs have been devised. The treble and bass clef signs shown above and the moveable C clef sign are the most commonly used clef signs today.

Meter signatures evolved through several systems to the present plan of marking off measures and indicating the corresponding beat and note unit in the signature.

old sign
for triple meter

half circle
old sign
for duple meter

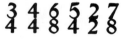

examples of
standard meter
signatures

In early music the ♭ sign indicated a lowered tone and ♯ indicated a raised tone. From these the key signature developed and is used to indicate the scale from which a melody takes most of its notes. Today when many composers write music on all twelve tones of the chromatic scale rather than on eight, key signatures often are omitted and the signs placed with the notes.

The standard notation we use today has developed through many systems from ancient times. Therefore it never was designed in a scientific way, and it is very limited. Its main features were fixed when music was much simpler than it is today. Today's composers often must find new symbols for communicating their ideas to performers of their music. Of the compositions you studied on pages 21 to 31, which could not have been written in standard notation?

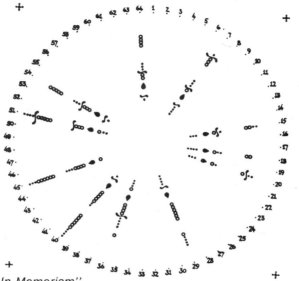

"Excerpt from *In Memoriam*" . . .
Crazy Horse (Symphony) by Robert Ashley
(1930-   , USA)

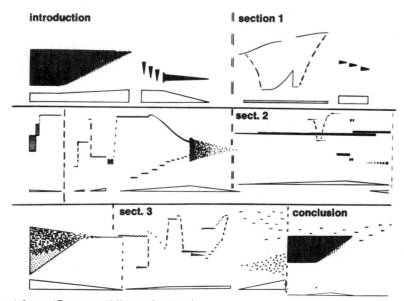

"Excerpt from *'Fragment'*," an electronic
composition by George Balch Wilson
(1927-   , USA)

experiments in music I

Fully explore the "non-traditional" ways of producing sounds on the guitar.

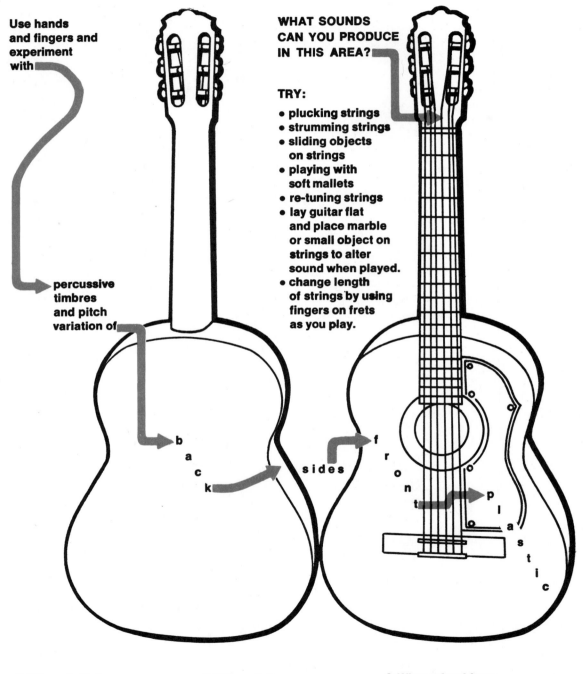

Use hands and fingers and experiment with

percussive timbres and pitch variation of

b
a
c
k

s i d e s

WHAT SOUNDS CAN YOU PRODUCE IN THIS AREA?

TRY:
- **plucking strings**
- **strumming strings**
- **sliding objects on strings**
- **playing with soft mallets**
- **re-tuning strings**
- **lay guitar flat and place marble or small object on strings to alter sound when played.**
- **change length of strings by using fingers on frets as you play.**

f
r
o
n
t

p
l
a
s
t
i
c

? Where is high _____

? Where is low _____

? What other ideas _____

what?

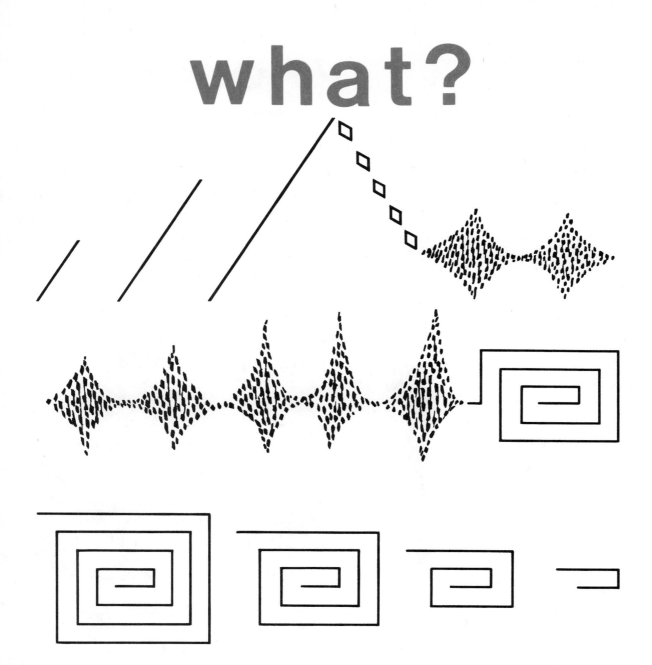

Can you read the score above? Find a way to interpret each symbol as accurately as possible on the guitar. Include the new sounds you discovered. Practice the composition until you play it well. Tape your performance. In class compare your tape with tapes of other class members.

Compose a piece called "Two Performers and One Guitar." Work in twos and plan your composition. Select the sounds you will use and organize them. Invent a symbol for each block of sound. Write notation for your composition. In class share some of the compositions, and if possible, project the notation for the class to see.

the sound of soul

Many have tried to describe what "soul" really is. Otis Redding, a Black singer popular in the 60's, defined it this way:

> "Soul is something that you really have to bring up from your heart; it's not something that you can just think of. It's really something that you think of and you get in mind and you <u>see</u> it and you <u>feel</u> it, and you <u>say</u> it just right—and really <u>mean</u> it—that's soul."

The music of the American Negro is one of the most unique elements in the development of America. Blues and the spiritual are the folk music of the American Negro, and jazz developed from these. The blues are solo songs which sprang from everyday life. Blues songs are accompanied by guitar, piano, or other instruments. Spirituals are choral, intensely religious, and originally were performed without accompaniment. Black gospel music has been a part of the church service for many years. It is characterized by spirited group singing and a unique style of organ and piano playing. For more than a hundred years, Black music—blues, work songs, spirituals, jazz, gospel songs, and soul—has remained a strong and developing American art.

Wade in the Water

Spiritual
Arr. B. A. R.

2.

God's a - gon - na trou - ble the wa - ter. ___ Now

God's a - gon - na trou - ble the wa - ter. ___

Wade ___ in the wa - ter. ___

Wade ___ in the wa - ter. ___

Jor - dan's wa - ter is ___ chil - ly and cold, ___
you ___ get there ___ be - fore ___ I do, ___

Wa - ter, ___ wa - ter, ___

Wa - ter, ___ wa - ter, ___

Wa - ter, ___ wa - ter, ___

(All)   (Solo)

God's a - gon - na trou - ble the wa - ter, ___ It

God's a - gon - na trou - ble the wa - ter, ___ Just

Wade ___ in the wa - ter, ___

Wade ___ in the wa - ter. ___

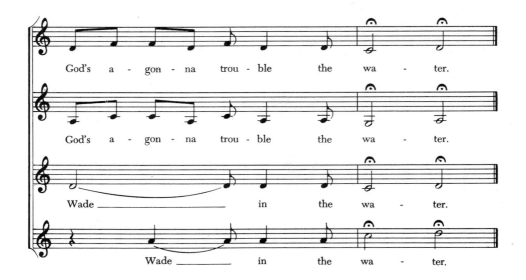

God's a - gon - na trou - ble the wa - ter.

God's a - gon - na trou - ble the wa - ter.

Wade _____ in the wa - ter.

Wade _____ in the wa - ter.

The melody is based on this pentatonic scale:

Build your own arrangement by first using the vocal parts provided here. Part 1 is the melody. Part 2 is a harmonizing part. Part 3 is an ostinato to be sung in any octave. Part 4 is written as a vocal descant, but it may be played on an instrument. You may make up other parts of your own—instrumental as well as vocal—by improvising with the notes of the pentatonic scale. Follow the style of the parts given here. Any combination of the five notes will make effective harmony with the pentatonic melody.

As previously stated, "soul" is many things. You may perform this song with various "sounds of soul." You may sing the vocal parts given here, or, by simply changing the rhythmic structure, you may change the stylistic feeling of the song. Listen to the recording for a demonstration of this. The song is first presented with the vocal parts accompanied by Afro-Cuban patterns. Then instruments perform in gospel and soul styles. During the instrumental version, you may sing the vocal parts given here or other parts of your own. For an example of "Wade in the Water" jazz style, see page 82.

Here are examples of how you may perform some of the "sounds of soul."

AFRO-CUBAN
Moderately fast tempo

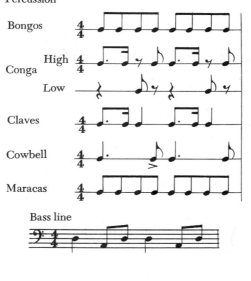

GOSPEL
Moderately slow tempo

SOUL
Fast, driving tempo

Go Down Moses

Spiritual
Arr. B. A. R.

God's Goin' to Set This World on Fire

Spiritual
Arranged by William Grant Still

God's goin' to set this world on fi -
yah, God's goin' to set this world on fi - yah One of these
days, Hal - le - lu - jah! God's goin' to set this world on fi -
yah, God's goin' to set this world on fi - yah one of these days.

Descant

I'm goin' to climb up Ja - cob's lad - der, I'm goin' to

Melody

climb up Ja - cob's lad - der on - a that day, Hal - le - lu - jah! I'm goin' to

climb up Ja - cob's lad - der, I'm goin' to climb up Ja - cob's

lad - der on - a that day. God don't

want no cow - ard sol - diers, God don't want no cow - ard

gradually slower

sol - diers none of these days, Hal - le - lu - jah! God don't want no cow - ard

slower

sol - diers, God don't want no cow- ard sol-diers none of these days. ___

An American Composer

William Grant Still (1895-   )

William Grant Still fully deserves the title "Dean of Negro Composers," for his career has spanned the century, and he continues to compose, lecture, and conduct. On a radio broadcast of music composed by Americans, the composer once said, "This music should speak to the hearts of every one of you, for it comes from the hearts of the men who wrote it." His statement certainly can be applied to his own music. Growing up in the South, Still was surrounded in childhood by the music of his people. His parents were musical and Still, while he was a youngster, developed the aspiration to be a composer.

Still had learned to play the violin, and in college he played in a string quartet. He arranged music for the group to play. He led the band and arranged for it. He learned to play the clarinet and other instruments including the piccolo and saxophone. This knowledge of instruments helped him later in writing music for orchestra. Still studied composition with fine teachers, and he experimented with several styles of composing. But, as a young man, he made the firm decision to adopt the music of Negroes as the basis for his musical style and to use titles referring to the Negro. In his fifty or more compositions, he stayed with this decision.

Scherzo *(Humor)*

from *Afro-American Symphony*

by William Grant Still

The *Afro-American Symphony,* written in 1931, is the first symphony composed by an American Negro. In describing the third movement, Still commented, "It is saying 'Hallelujah!' " Listen to the movement and study the main theme. Notice the "Hallelujah" motive and the reason for Still's subtitle "Humor." In the movement you will hear an introduction, sections based on the principal theme, episodes, and a coda.

MAIN THEME

O Happy Day

Words and Music
by Edwin Hawkins

Improvise in a manner similar to the recording. Use these patterns for an introduction and on the ad-lib section.

Hand clapping is an essential part of Black gospel music, coming from the tradition of spirituals and African folk music. Improvise with these patterns, and make up others during the introduction and ad-lib section.

Vocal embellishment is also a basic part of gospel style. Here are the first six bars with embellishment.

I Wish I Knew How It Would Feel to Be Free

Music by Billy Taylor
Words by Billy Taylor and Dick Dallas
Arr. B. A. R.

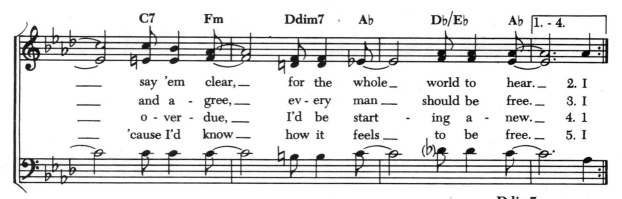

| C7 | Fm | | Ddim7 · | Ab | Db/Eb | Ab | 1. - 4. |

say 'em clear, __ for the whole_ world to hear. _ 2. I
and a - gree, __ ev - ery man __ should be free. _ 3. I
o - ver - due, __ I'd be start - ing a - new. _ 4. 1
'cause I'd know __ how it feels __ to be free. _ 5. I

5.   *f*   >   C7   *ritard.*   Fm   Ddim7

Say 'em loud, _ say 'em clear, _____ for the

f

Ab   Db/Ab   Ab

whole wide world to hear. _____

Billy Taylor

elements of jazz

The sound of jazz dates from the end of the last century. Invented and first played and sung by the American Negro, jazz is genuinely unique music which has grown and developed continuously. It has been one of the richest and most vital forces of our musical heritage. Today we hear elements of jazz in classical composed music; we hear many new uses of the elements as they are mixed with other styles of popular music; and we hear the traditional jazz of earlier periods. Radio and recordings bring us performances of New Orleans Dixieland jazz recorded in the early 1900's, and some entertainers of today specialize in "Trad" (traditional) jazz, playing in the early style. We often hear various styles dating from 1900: Ragtime, Boogie Woogie, Swing, Bop, Cool, Funky, Progressive, and Third Stream. Today, jazz is international, and is performed and heard in countries around the world.

The elements that give jazz a unique sound are derived from many sources. The blues made a large contribution. From the blues with its blue notes we get a scale that might be called the "jazz scale."

Blue notes

In some styles of jazz the blues song structure is adopted as the form.

The element of rhythm furnishes the driving pulse of jazz. Drums, the string bass, guitar, or piano hold the music together and give it vitality through a strong rhythmic beat. Syncopation has a special place in jazz, with the strong accent being placed on normally weak beats.

A variety of tone colors is among the most unusual qualities of jazz. An instrument often imitates the jazz singer. Vibrato, growls, and rasps are used. Mutes give different colors.

Improvisation is a main element of jazz. The players are free to add ornaments, bend some of the notes, and make variations on the melody. It is a cooperative effort. As one player presents a new or altered pattern, the others must be ready to accommodate it.

You are already familiar with various versions of "Wade in the Water." Now listen to an interpretation by a jazz group playing piano, bass, guitar, and drums. On your recording you will hear the rhythm, melody, and harmony played straight and then the jazz version of each. Listen to the original rhythm (example 1), the original harmony (example 2), and the original melody (example 3). Notice what happens in the jazz rhythm (example 4), the jazz harmony (example 5), and the melody with improvisation (example 6). Then follow the complete jazz performance of "Wade in the Water," and notice the jazz elements throughout.

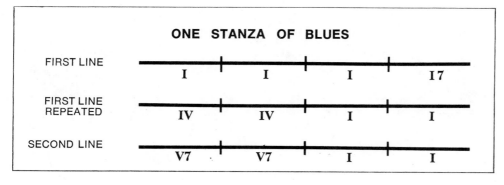

	ONE STANZA OF BLUES			
FIRST LINE	I	I	I	I 7
FIRST LINE REPEATED	IV	IV	I	I
SECOND LINE	V7	V7	I	I

Example no. 1, rhythm

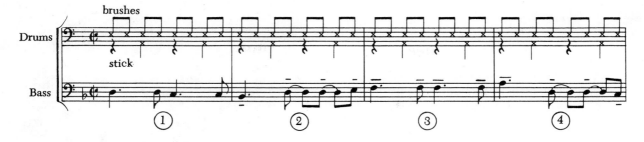

Drums — brushes / stick

Bass — ① ② ③ ④

Example no. 2, harmony

Guitar

Dm | B♭ Dm | F | Am Dm

① ② ③ ④

Example no. 3, melody

Piano — in chords

Dm | B♭ Dm | F | Am Dm

① ② ③ ④

Example no. 4, improvised rhythm

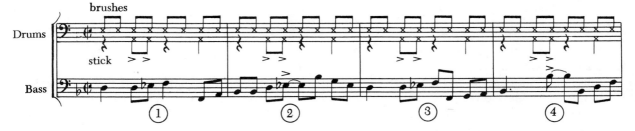

Drums — brushes / stick

Bass — ① ② ③ ④

Example no. 5, improvised harmony

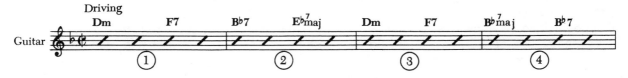

Guitar — Driving

Dm | F7 | B♭7 | E♭maj7 | Dm | F7 | B♭maj7 | B♭7

① ② ③ ④

Example no. 6, improvised melody

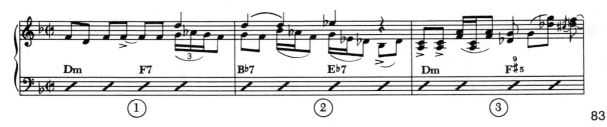

Dm | F7 | B♭7 | E♭7 | Dm | F♯9#5

① ② ③

It's About That Time (Excerpt)

Played by Miles Davis (1926-   , USA)

Jazz has passed through many styles since it first became a musical form used for dancing before the turn of the century. As music for entertainment, it continues to develop and to be a vital form. Today many new elements are heard. Performances of the popular entertainer, Miles Davis, are sometimes called "jazz of the future." In "It's About That Time" the form is free rather than fixed as in early jazz. The sounds of rock are fused with other sounds in the melody and rhythm. The harmony consists of many tones not included in the fundamental chords. New instruments are used. As you listen, discover all the new sounds. Discover which elements of early jazz are retained. What special interest do you find in **texture** in this jazz performance?

Rhapsody in Blue, Second Section

by George Gershwin (1898-1937, USA)

This composition is as American as movies, baseball, rodeos, and hamburgers. And it is an American success story. Jazz rhythms and blues melodies were everywhere around the young Gershwin in the twenties. He was a fine jazzman himself, playing jazz piano and composing popular songs. It bothered him that many educated people and other musicians of the time felt jazz to be nothing more than dance music. Gershwin said that in writing *Rhapsody in Blue* he had the strong resolve and main purpose of trying to prove that jazz had no such limitation and of giving it the dignity of serious music.

No effort ever was more phenomenally successful. Gershwin himself played the piano for the first performance in 1924 with Paul Whiteman's orchestra. The music gained instant recognition. Very soon it was heard on radio, in concerts, in arrangements for every type of band and orchestra, for ballet, and in numerous other forms. At once it brought Gershwin great fame. More important, the work was a landmark in musical history, setting a new trend. Composers in many parts of the world began using jazz rhythms and melodies in their compositions. Jazz was acknowledged as a form of great music.

Gershwin said that often he heard music in the heart of noise and that this music was conceived as he rode a train "with its steely rhythms, its rattly bang." Indeed, we can easily hear that this is music of the age of steel, of building cities, of jazz—the time of the twenties in America. The second section of *Rhapsody in Blue* is on your recording. It begins with the melody featured as the main theme of the composition. Discuss the jazz sounds and Gershwin's individual style of composing. Why is the title appropriate for the work?

Competition and Galop

from *Fancy Free*

by Leonard Bernstein (1918-   , USA)

Composers have used the sounds of jazz in their music for the Broadway stage and ballet to make it sound truly American. The composer of the ballet *Fancy Free* is well known to young people through his *West Side Story* and televised lecture-concerts. In one scene of *Fancy Free*, three sailors on leave in New York compete for dates with two girls. After the three scramble to dance with the girls, each sailor in turn does a solo dance to impress them. The music on your record accompanies first the amusing antics of the three-way competition, and then the boisterous, happy-go-lucky dance of the first sailor. The syncopated rhythms, off-beat accents, changing meters, "blues" piano, and street sounds all contribute to the distinctive "Americana" sound of Bernstein's music.

"Pour le ragtime d'Igor Stravinsky" design by Pablo Picasso, Courtesy French Reproduction Rights and Les Editions Recontre Lausanne et La Guilde De Disque

What strands of jazz composition can you see in this serigraph?

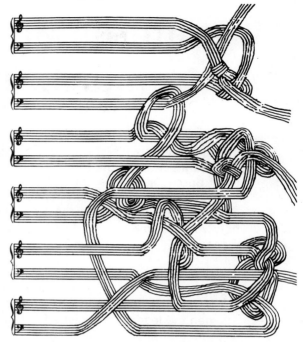

"Jazz," Serigraph by Bob Gill, 1963, Roko Gallery, New York

Ebony Concerto

First and Second Movements

by Igor Stravinsky (1882-1971, Russia, USA)

Stravinsky was a prolific composer who wrote monumental works for orchestra, ballet, chamber groups, and the stage. From early youth, he was influenced by the sounds of jazz. This work is concert music, but the elements of jazz are heard throughout.

Ebony Concerto is for clarinet and jazz band. Listen to each movement and discover the jazz elements. What do you hear of jazz rhythm, melody, harmony, and tone color? How is the music different from genuine jazz? What are the imaginative qualities that are the composer's own?

patterns and designs in music: imitation

Imitation is a musical device used by practically all composers. It may be an important aspect of the form, as in a fugue, canon, or invention. Or it may be used briefly, as echoes of different types furnish variety. The imitative passages may be in the same pitches or higher or lower. They may be rhythmic imitation only. It is fun to create imitation in musical sound, and doing so will help you become aware of it in music you hear or perform. Try these experiments.

1. Work in twos, each partner playing a different percussion instrument or sound-maker. Take turns being the leader and follower. Make a game of inventing rhythmic patterns and imitating them. The follower might begin when the leader has finished, or after four beats, one beat, etc. Invent patterns that are more and more complex.

2. Play two melody instruments similarly. Discover several ways to imitate pitches—exactly, backward, inverted, in a different key, with harmony tones added, and so on.

3. Perform rounds with spoken words. Choose a round from pages 89 to 91, and say the words instead of singing them. Develop voice pitches and distinctive tone qualities that result in harmony and interest.

4. Dramatize rounds in movement as you sing. Do different movements with each phrase of the song so that you have a round in movement as well as in sound.

5. Compose some original rounds to sing. Choose rhymes for your text or compose your own text. The number of measures must divide equally by the number of voices. The harmony may be built around the I and V chords by using tones of these chords in your melody. Or you may compose a "twentieth-century round" with more unusual harmony. Notice the harmonies of the rounds on pages 89 to 91. Use several sets of resonator bells to experiment as you decide on the melodies and harmonies for your rounds.

6. Compose instrumental rounds. Use percussion or melody instruments or a combination of the two.

Two-Part Invention in D Minor

by Johann Sebastian Bach (1685-1750, Germany)

The musical device of imitation appears in music of all times, but the polyphonic music of the eighteenth-century composer Bach is especially replete with it. In this invention the voice in treble, played by the right hand, usually is the leader, and the bass voice played by the left hand is the imitator.

Patterns of imitation can be seen in the notation below. Compare the bass part in measures 5 and 6 with the treble part in measures 3 and

4. Compare the treble part of measures 7, 8, 9, and 10 with the bass part of measures 13, 14, 15, and 16. As you listen to the invention, notice these and other passages in which imitation occurs.

For this lesson the recording is played on piano. Review the rendition on Moog Synthesizer (see page 30). Which musical element or quality is most affected by the different sound source?

Allegro

Symphony in B Flat for Concert Band

Third Movement (Fugue)

by Paul Hindemith (1895-1963, Germany, United States)

Listen first to this composition with the purpose of hearing and identifying the sounds of the wind instruments that make up the concert band. The composition is written for percussion section, bass and baritone horns, trombones (three parts), French horns (four parts), trumpets in B flat (two parts), cornets in B flat (three parts), solo cornet in B flat, baritone saxophone in E flat, tenor saxophone in B flat, alto saxophones in E flat (two parts), bassoons (two parts), bass clarinet in B flat, alto clarinet in E flat, clarinets in B flat (three parts), solo clarinet in B flat, clarinet in E flat, oboes (two parts), flutes (two parts), and piccolo. Hear the movement a second time and notice the melodies and the harmony which include many chromatic tones. Share your observations in a class summary of all that was heard in the music. At later times, study the design of the composition in detail.

The movement is a **fugue.** The principal musical material of a fugue is called a **subject.** The voices or parts of a fugue begin one after another, each opening with the subject in imitation.

This fugue by the contemporary composer, Hindemith, is in three sections, and it is a **double fugue** because it has two subjects which are eventually played at the same time. The first section features the first subject, and the second features the second subject, and in the third section the two subjects are combined. Play and sing the subjects until you know them well and then follow the outline of the fugue as you listen to it.

First Section

Nine-Measure introduction

First Subject (nine measures) stated by cornets, French horns and baritone horn (a fourth below); by oboes and E flat clarinet; by piccolo, flutes and B flat clarinet; and by baritone and bass horns.

Development (brief)—many entrances of the subject beginning on different tones, *scherzando* section with the woodwinds in prominence.

Second Section

Second Subject (five measures) stated by flute, bass clarinet, and bassoons; then by clarinets; by flutes; by oboes and E flat clarinet; and by cornets (false or incomplete statement).

Development (brief)—woodwinds in many entrances of Second Subject, *scherzando* with woodwind solos—free ending, fading out with a short flute solo.

Third Section

First and Second Subjects, played simultaneously.

Tallis' Canon

Music by Thomas Tallis
Words by Joseph Addison

1. The spacious firmament on high, With all the blue ethereal sky, And spangled heav'ns, a shining frame, Their great Original proclaim. The unwearied sun from day to day Does his Creator's power display, And publishes to every land The works of an almighty hand.

2. Soon as the evening shades prevail
   The moon takes up the wondrous tale,
   And nightly to the listening earth
   Repeats the story of her birth;
   Whilst all the stars that round her burn,
   And all the planets in their turn,
   Confirm the tidings, as they roll,
   And spread the truth from pole to pole.

3. What though in solemn silence, all
   Move round the dark terrestrial ball;
   What though nor real voice nor sound
   Amid their radiant orbs be found;
   In reason's ear they all rejoice,
   And utter forth a glorious voice;
   For ever singing as they shine,
   "The hand that made us is divine."

Come, Quiet Hour

German Round
Translation by B. L.

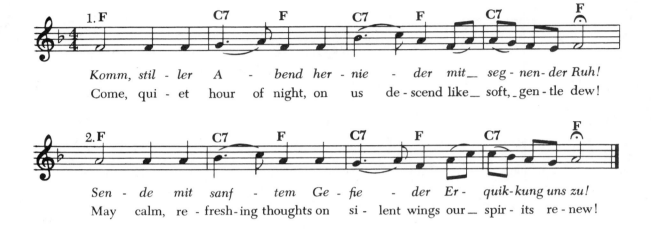

1. Komm, stil - ler A - bend her - nie - der mit_ seg - nen- der Ruh!
   Come, qui - et hour of night, on us de - scend like_ soft, _gen - tle dew!

2. Sen - de mit sanf - tem Ge - fie - der Er - quik- kung uns zu!
   May calm, re - fresh-ing thoughts on si - lent wings our_ spir - its re - new!

Melody and Harmony

by W. B. Bradbury

to line 2

1. It is pleas - ing to _ hear a one - voice mel - o - dy;

to line 3

2. Now with a sec - ond the_ mu - sic sweet - er still will be;

3. Then with a third voice we sing with rich - er har - mo - ny.

Shalom, Chaverim

Israeli Round

Sha - lom, cha - ve - rim! Sha - lom, cha - ve - rim! Sha - lom, sha - lom!
Fare - well, good _ friends, Fare - well, good _ friends, Fare - well, fare - well!

Le - hit - ra - ot, le - hit - ra - ot, Sha - lom, sha - lom!
Till we meet a - gain, till we meet a - gain, Fare - well, fare - well!

Einundzwanzig

German Round

1. Ein - und - zwan - zig, zwei - und - zwan - zig, drei und vier und fünf und sechs - und -
Sie - ben - und - zwan - zig, acht - und - zwan - zig, neun - und - zwan - zig _ und _

zwan - zig.
dreis - sig. O lee ay lee o, o lee ay lee o.

2. Einunddreissig . . .   6. Einundsiebzig . . .

3. Einundvierzig . . .   7. Einundachtzig . . .

4. Einundfünfzig . . .   8. Einundneunzig . . . und hundert

5. Einundsechzig . . .

music
of the
guitar

The modern guitar is derived from the Spanish vihuela de mano of the sixteenth century. The vihuela had the same popularity in Renaissance Spain as did the lute in other countries. At that time both instruments had double strings, and they were tuned alike. They were played to accompany ballads and dances. From about 1750 to 1850 the guitar was a popular instrument in England and America, and in those years considerable literature was composed for the instrument. In recent times it has been again a most popular folk and concert instrument.

Mounsier's Almaine

Variations on a Dance Tune

by Daniell Batchelar

In its original form for lute, this composition appeared in a book in England in 1610. It has been a common practice to transcribe lute music for the guitar. Theme and variations has been a favorite design for showing off the possibilities of an instrument and the virtuosity of the performer. This little composition seems to have that purpose. The dance tune follows.

Early lute

When you have enjoyed the sounds of the guitar and the overall character of the piece several times, analyze the musical content more precisely. Discover how many variations are played. Use a form like that on page 56, and complete an outline of important features in each variation.

As you work, find answers for these questions.

1. Which variation is the most strongly syncopated?

2. In which are scale patterns used as ornamental notes?

3. In which are repetitions of one note used as ornaments?

4. How did the composer close the composition?

5. In which do you hear the guitar imitate the sound of the two sets of strings of the lute?

Prelude No. 2 in E Major

by Heitor Villa-Lobos (1887-1959, Brazil)

The Brazilian composer Villa-Lobos wrote several compositions for guitar including a concerto. In this prelude what typical guitar sounds do you hear? What common design is used in the work? How did the composer achieve the elements of variety and unity within this design?

Pantheistic Study for Guitar and Large Bird

by Chad Stuart

Like other performers and composers, this contemporary pop musician finds improvisation well suited to the guitar. His title is meant to imply relationship to nature. Pantheism is a doctrine which identifies God with nature.

How do Chad Stuart's improvisations reflect his musical interests and the time in which he lives? How is the "large bird" represented musically?

Make a skeleton diagram of what you hear in the music, and fill it in as you listen to the music several times. Indicate the six sections on your paper. With words or symbols indicate what takes place in each section. Use arrows or other symbols to show relationships of the different sections. Show when the element of surprise is heard. Indicate any musical material that is heard more than once.

When you have completed the detailed diagram, reduce it to a simple one using only letters of the alphabet or some other symbols. Discuss the elements and qualities of music (page 32) as they are heard in this work.

Alegria del Alosno

Spanish Folk Melody

Flamenco music is most widely played in Andalusia in southern Spain where the gypsy flamenco tradition began. Flamenco dancers with their exciting foot work are familiar entertainers. The guitar, which allows for a great deal of improvisation, always has been the instrument of flamenco music.

93

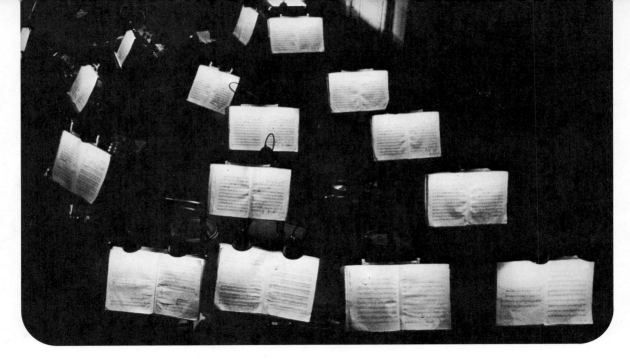

instruments of the band and orchestra

Instruments of the band and orchestra are of continuing importance to students of music. There are several different aspects to the study of instruments. Each is of interest, and each contributes to better understanding of musical sound. As you study instruments and the music produced on them, explore the following.

1. The tone color or timbre of each instrument —the sound by which it is distinguished from all the other instruments.

2. The combinations of instruments that result in still other interesting and colorful sounds.

3. The range of tones that can be produced on each instrument.

4. The playing techniques that produce different sounds.

5. The characteristic ways in which a composer uses instrumental sounds as a part of his own style of writing music.

6. The history of each instrument, when it came into common use, how it was developed.

7. The instruments in each historic era and ways in which they were used in musical compositions of the time.

Plan some explorations that will help you become better acquainted with musical instruments and more aware of instrumental sounds in the music you study. Invite players of percussion, brass, woodwind, and string instruments to play for you and to demonstrate the various playing techniques. If possible, hold many of the instruments yourselves. Practice the technique of bowing a violin or cello. Practice the technique of blowing a clarinet, flute, or oboe. See films that give you more information about playing and listening to instruments. Find books in the library that give information about the instruments.

Symphony for Band, Opus 69

Fourth Movement

by Vincent Persichetti (1915-   )

The prominent American composer Vincent Persichetti has written several compositions for symphonic band. In the fourth movement of his *Symphony for Band* he contrasts the tone colors of the woodwind, brass, and percussion groups and also features solo instruments. The movement is in extended **rondo** form, with an introduction and a **coda.**

The composition opens with the woodwinds playing the rondo or main theme. It consists only of six sharp, **staccato** chords. At the end of this introduction the snare drum plays the rhythm of the opening theme. The main part of the movement begins with a forceful statement of the rondo theme played by the brass.

The design of the composition is as follows:

Introduction

A—rondo theme played by brass

B—short melody played by high woodwinds with this rhythm:

A—repeated

C—brief oboe solo

A—repeated

D—legato melody played by clarinets

A—rondo theme used as bridge

E—melody played by clarinets (similar to Theme D)

Free section—rondo theme in combination with fragments of other themes

Coda—new melodic ideas. Near the end, a fragment of rondo theme played by brass. Final brilliant chord containing all the tones of the chromatic scale.

TYPICAL SEATING PLAN OF A BAND

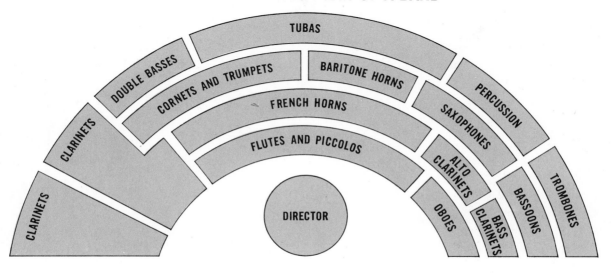

TUBA

Approximate Sounding Range of Common Brass Instruments

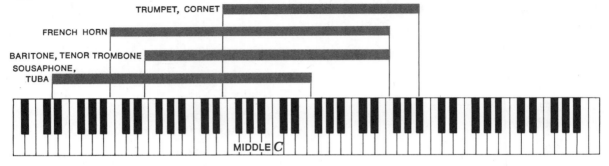

TRUMPET, CORNET

FRENCH HORN

BARITONE, TENOR TROMBONE

SOUSAPHONE,
TUBA

MIDDLE *C*

TENOR TROMBONE
BARITONE

TRUMPET
CORNET

FRENCH HORN

SOUSAPHONE

Heroic Music

Honor, Bravery, Vigor,
Playfulness, Joy

by Georg Philipp Telemann (1681-1767)

Telemann wrote countless numbers of compositions. It was said that he could write intricate music as easily as one might write a letter. He had a gift for writing melodies, and he developed the idea of descriptive "tone painting" in music.

Telemann composed a series of marches describing the various aspects of the character of an opera hero. The little compositions are played by a brass ensemble of two trumpets and two trombones, percussion instruments (mainly timpani), and organ. The trumpets are featured throughout the marches.

The Trumpet

The trumpet has been a part of the history of man from earliest times. Trumpets have been found in Egyptian tombs of the fourteenth century B. C. The Bible contains many references to the instrument. The first trumpets, called "natural" trumpets, were simple tubes that could produce only a few tones blown above one fundamental pitch. That one pitch would designate the "key" of the instrument. All brass instruments originally were of this type. At about the time Telemann was composing, **crooks** were added to the instruments. These pieces of tubing made the instrument longer and therefore able to produce a lower fundamental pitch and a different set of related tones.

The present-day trumpet has valves which automatically add lengths of tubing, the crooks, to the basic length of the instrument. Its natural tone (when no valves are pressed) is usually B flat. The role of the trumpet today is more varied than ever before. The influence of jazz performers can be noticed in greater agility in playing technique and in the use of the extremes of high and low register.

Telemann was a contemporary of Bach and Handel. His musical style is of the Baroque era, and the trumpets played in these compositions are baroque trumpets in D. As you listen to the marches, discover answers to these questions.

By what musical means did the composer describe the five different qualities of his hero?

The marches are all in two-part or three-part design. In which design is each march?

What different echo effects do you hear in the marches?

How many different pitches are played on the timpani?

In which march is another percussion instrument featured?

Approximate Sounding Range of Common Woodwind Instruments

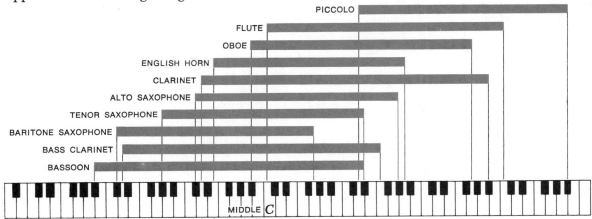

PICCOLO
FLUTE
OBOE
ENGLISH HORN
CLARINET
ALTO SAXOPHONE
TENOR SAXOPHONE
BARITONE SAXOPHONE
BASS CLARINET
BASSOON

MIDDLE *C*

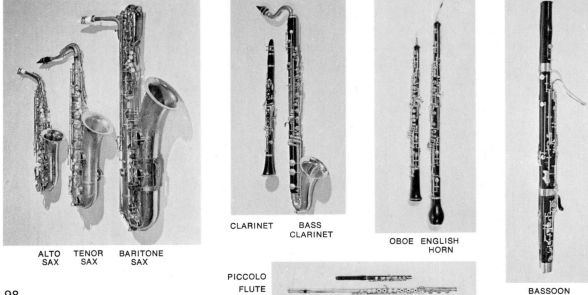

CLARINET   BASS
CLARINET

OBOE ENGLISH
HORN

ALTO   TENOR   BARITONE
SAX   SAX   SAX

PICCOLO
FLUTE

BASSOON

Kleine Kammermusik, Opus 24, No. 2

Third Movement

by Paul Hindemith (1895-1963)

A favorite instrumental ensemble of twentieth-century composers is known as the woodwind quintet even though one instrument of the group is a member of the brass family. The range and tone quality of the French horn used in combination with those of the flute, oboe, clarinet, and bassoon, offers many possibilities for interesting compositions. With books closed, first listen to the third movement of this "Little Chamber Music" to enjoy the sounds of the instruments in the quintet. Listen to the recording again and listen especially for the musical ideas of which the music was composed. Discover themes, rhythmic interest, harmony, and design. Discover ideas that have been used in music by many composers of different eras and those which seem to belong to this twentieth-century composer. Later, study the music in detail and complete your analysis.

THEME ONE

THEME TWO

LISTENING EXPLORATION

Think of the sustained melodies of section one as a series of question-answer phrases. Analyze the effective use of melodic direction and instrumentation. In the second section of the composition this pattern of rhythm becomes an **ostinato** accompaniment:

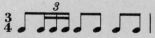

Which instruments play it? Which play the melody of this section? Why does the beginning of the theme of this section remind us of Theme One? Describe the bridge passage that leads to the third section of the composition.

Throughout the composition, notice the special sound of the harmony which accompanies the melodies, the alternating major and minor sounds, and the intervals between pairs of instruments playing the same melody.

VIOLIN   VIOLA   CELLO   DOUBLE BASS

Approximate Sounding Range of Bowed String Instruments

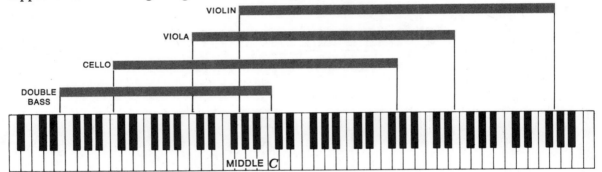

VIOLIN

VIOLA

CELLO

DOUBLE BASS

MIDDLE *C*

Range of the Harp

String Quartet in C Major, Opus 76, No. 3
Second Movement

by Joseph Haydn (1732-1809)

This movement in theme and variations is considered to be one of the most exquisite compositions for the string quartet. The theme is a hymn melody composed by Haydn and adopted as the Austrian National Anthem. The hymn is still sung in many churches. You may have sung it with words that begin "Glorious things of thee are spoken, Zion, city of our God." Listen to the theme as it is first presented in slow tempo. Four variations follow. With your books closed listen to the entire movement. Discuss all that you hear in the music. Later study the movement in more detail using the ideas below to complete your analysis.

Variation I

The second violin plays the melody. Which instrument plays the staccato countermelody? Since the other two instruments are silent, what kind of instrumental duet is the variation?

Variation II

Which instrument plays the melody in this variation? A new countermelody is played by the second violin. Describe the accompaniment part played by the first violin.

Variation III

The viola plays the melody. How is the winding legato effect achieved in the accompaniment?

Variation IV

The theme is treated in chorale or hymn style with four-part harmony. The melody is played by the first violin for the first time since the original statement of the theme. No vibrato is used in playing the melody at the beginning of the variation, and an interesting effect is created. The melody is then played an octave higher, and vibrato is used. The use of these special tone qualities of the violin and the close harmony give an ethereal sound. A brief coda brings the movement to a close.

Gaucho Serenade

by Ennio Bolognini (1893-   , Argentina)

This unusual music for cello was composed by an Argentine cellist to show off the possibilities of the unaccompanied instrument when played pizzicato. How do the instrumental sounds make the title seem appropriate?

Do some independent study on the string quartet.

In what ways is the term "string quartet" used? Which instrument of the string family of the orchestra does not play in the group? What do the terms "first violin" and "second violin" mean?

Study items 1 and 5 on page 94 in relation to the instruments of the string quartet.

CYMBALS   TEMPLE BLOCKS
BASS DRUM   GONG   SNARE DRUM

MARACAS   TRIANGLE   WOOD BLOCKS   TAMBOURINE   TRAP SET
                CLAVES   CASTANETS   GUIRO

ORCHESTRA BELLS   CHIMES   XYLOPHONE   CELESTA
MARIMBA   VIBRAPHONE   TIMPANI

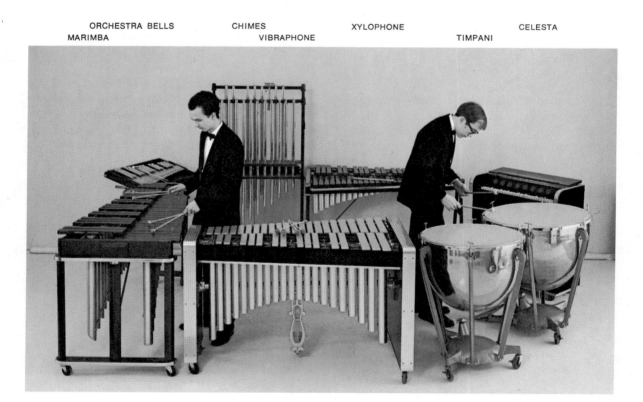

Sounds from the Percussion Section

The percussion family is probably the oldest of the instrumental groups. The instruments were used a great deal in early music. The percussion section of the band and orchestra is favored by some composers of today, and whole compositions are written for percussion instruments alone. Listen again to the fourth movement of *Symphony for Band* by Vincent Persichetti, a composer of today, and notice especially the sounds of the percussion instruments. Listen to *Heroic Music* by Telemann who was writing music in the year 1700. What percussion instruments do you hear? How are the percussion sounds different in these two compositions?

Sketch for Percussion

by Ronald Lo Presti (1933-　, USA)

This recent composition features contrasts of the delicate sounds of the celesta, marimba, and piano against the clamor of the xylophone, timpani, snare drum, bass drum, gong, triangle, and suspended cymbal. As you listen, discover how many instruments of the percussion family you can identify. How did the composer achieve a satisfying piece of music with these instruments alone? Give your answer in terms of the elements and qualities of all music (page 32).

The Timpani

The timpani, or kettledrums, are exceptionally useful and expressive percussion instruments because they can produce pitched tones. The drums, usually played in pairs, are basin-shaped shells of copper with heads of calfskin or some other material. By manually turning screws around the edge of the drumhead, or by a more modern mechanical device which does the same thing by means of foot pedals, the skin can be tightened or loosened to raise or lower the pitch.

Using two drums is a very old idea. For early military music in Asia and in the European Cavalry, drums were played in pairs, one resting on either side of the camel or horse. The idea was taken to England at the time of the Crusades. Kettledrums are referred to in the Bible and in Shakespearean literature. They have been important in music of composers from the sixteen hundreds to the present.

Until the middle of the eighteenth century, one of the kettledrums was small, playing the tonic or first tone of a scale; the other was larger, playing four steps below the tonic on the fifth of the scale. In music by composers up to and including Beethoven, we hear these two pitches again and again in the timpani parts. Today, because of the tuning mechanism, the timpani can quickly produce a variety of pitches. The instrument is also capable of variety in timbre and dynamics. It contributes in many ways to music of the orchestra as well as to music of ensembles.

Ranges of Pitched Percussion Instruments

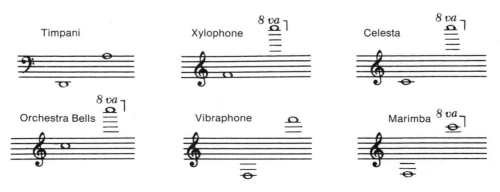

Boléro

by Maurice Ravel (1875-1937)

Boléro by Maurice Ravel is a good example of the importance a composer can place on instrumentation. The orchestration and dynamics are largely responsible for the interest this music holds. The composition is based on one rhythmic pattern repeated throughout and two forms of one melodic idea. Yet the composition takes fifteen minutes to play, because it is composed of eighteen repetitions of the dance tune. As you listen to the recording, use the notation below and the chart of the orchestration to study the composition.

MELODY A

MELODY B

When you know the music, study and discuss these problems.

1. Which instruments heard in the composition are not standard instruments of the orchestra? (Review pages 94 through 103 of your textbook.)

2. Look up the meaning of the terms **instrumentation, orchestration,** and **dynamics,** and discuss their meanings.

3. How are the two forms (A and B) of Ravel's melody alike and how different?

4. Review items 1 and 2 on page 94, and discuss them in relation to the instruments you hear in Ravel's *Boléro*.

5. From the diagram learn the usual seating arrangement of the symphony orchestra so that you will be able to locate the instruments easily when you attend concerts.

Chart of Orchestration of *Boléro*

Melody A

1. Solo Flute
2. Solo Clarinet

5. Solo Oboe D'Amore
6. Flute and Muted Trumpet

9. Piccolo, Flute, French Horn, Celesta
10. Oboe, Oboe D'Amore, English Horn, Clarinets

13. High Woodwinds and First Violins
14. High Woodwinds (including Tenor Saxophone), First and Second Violins

17. Piccolo, Flutes, Soprano and Tenor Saxophones, Trumpets (including Trumpet in D), First Violins

Coda: A short concluding passage for complete orchestra, with *glissandos* by Trombones

Melody B

3. Solo Bassoon
4. Small E♭ Clarinet

7. Solo Tenor Saxophone
8. Solo Sopranino Saxophone (Soprano Saxophone for last 3 measures)

11. Solo Trombone
12. High Woodwinds (including Tenor Saxophone)

15. High Woodwinds, Trumpet, First and Second Violins
16. High Woodwinds (including Soprano Saxophone), Trombone, Strings without Double Bass

18. Piccolo, Flutes, all Trumpets, Trombone, First Violins

Summary of Design of Boléro

$$\frac{1\text{-}2}{A} \Big/ \frac{3\text{-}4}{B} \Big/ \frac{5\text{-}6}{A} \Big/ \frac{7\text{-}8}{B} \Big/ \frac{9\text{-}10}{A} \Big/ \frac{11\text{-}12}{B} \Big/ \frac{13\text{-}14}{A} \Big/ \frac{15\text{-}16}{B} \Big/ \frac{17\text{-}18}{A \;\; B} \Big/ \quad \text{CODA}$$

TYPICAL SEATING PLAN OF A LARGE ORCHESTRA

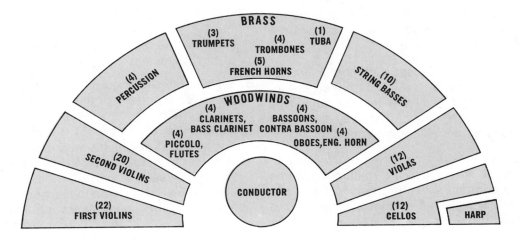

Symphony No. 4 in F Minor, Opus 36

Fourth Movement

by Peter Ilyich Tchaikovsky (1840-1893)

In the last movement of this popular symphony, we hear the entire range of orchestral sound. The orchestra is used as a brilliant **virtuoso** instrument. The music begins with a burst of sound from the entire orchestra. Strings and woodwinds play the downward scale patterns of the first theme as drums, clashing cymbals, and brass instruments play at full volume. The second theme, the melody of a folk song, is heard at once. The third theme follows immediately after a repetition of Theme One.

THEME ONE

THEME TWO

THEME THREE

1. Listen to the movement, and discuss all that you hear in the first playing.

2. Study the music in detail. How do you explain the idea that the folk melody is the real "star" of the composition? Which instruments play the folk theme and repetitions of it? Which instruments play accompaniments, countermelodies, or **embellishments** with this theme? How did the composer use the first phrase of the folk theme to build the climax of the composition?

3. Discuss the composer's choice of instruments. Why do you think he chose the instruments that play the folk melody? Why did he choose those that play the other themes and accompaniment parts?

4. Discuss the use of rhythm and melody in the music. How does the rhythm of Theme Three contrast with the rhythm of the folk theme? How is the rhythm of Theme One different from the others? What is the effect of the shimmering sound made by the violins when they play quick, repeated notes? What is the effect of the sound of the trombones when they play the notes of the folk theme in a sequence higher and higher? What are the feeling responses of the listener? Notice other melodic and rhythmic patterns played on a particular instrument, and discuss their musical purposes and effects.

5. How are the three themes used at the end of the movement?

6. On the opposite page, study the conductor's score for a portion of this composition beginning with measure 5. Study the abbreviations for the names of the instruments. Notice the order of the instruments in the score. Look at the part for each instrument. Locate the second part of Theme One. Locate Theme Two. Listen to this portion of the music on your recording several times, and follow the parts of the different instruments.

Excerpt from Tchaikovsky Symphony No. 4 in F Minor, Opus 36

american
folk songs
today and
yesterday

Songs Americans sing and have sung are from many sources. Early in our history the settlers sang those songs they remembered from their homelands. As national groups from around the world were represented in America, songs from everywhere became a part of our folk heritage. But from the beginning Americans sang their own songs, as well. The pioneering life, work, worship, and humor were subjects for folk songs. The tale of our nation's development is well told in her song literature.

Expression of feelings and thoughts in song is a continuing expression. Today songs continue to express important and trivial conditions, emotions, and events. Whereas earlier folk songs often were the creations of unknown individuals or groups, many such songs of today are composed by pop singers, composers, or poets who are identified. Yet the folk character of the music and words and the widespread popularity of the songs entitles them to be called folk songs. Along with old and new songs in the category of folk, are new performances of old songs. Often the text or music or both are somewhat changed in the new version. The performance style may be very modern and may be identified with a particular performer or group.

On the following pages is a sampling of American folk songs, old and new, and some old ones given a new sound. The original "Wayfarin' Stranger" and a modern arrangement of it follow. "Wanderin'" appears in the original form and in an arrangement. "He's Gone Away" and "Whoopee Ti-Yi-Yo" are typical historical folk songs while "Joy Is Like the Rain," and "The Power and Glory" are composed folk songs of the present. Balladeers are represented by people such as Woody Guthrie and Buffy Sainte-Marie.

Wayfarin' Stranger

American Folk Song
Adapted and Arr. B. A. R.

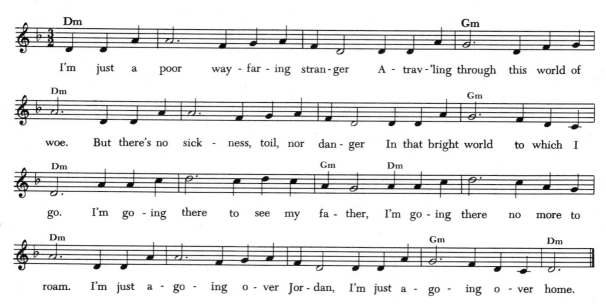

I'm just a poor way - far - ing stran - ger A - trav - 'ling through this world of woe. But there's no sick - ness, toil, nor dan - ger In that bright world to which I go. I'm go - ing there to see my fa - ther, I'm go - ing there no more to roam. I'm just a - go - ing o - ver Jor - dan, I'm just a - go - ing o - ver home.

The style of this arrangement might be called "folk-rock." The piano accompaniment contains the harmonic and rhythmic elements that suggest this style.

The chordal movement—bass line—is simple, yet the alternation between the G7 and Gm chords, and the A7 and C chords provides a modal feeling characteristic of many contemporary songs. The right hand provides a basic rhythmic flow of patterns in folk-rock style. In the first bar the use of the non-chord tone E is a type of embellishment often found in folk and country music.

1. I'm just a

110

home, I'm on - ly go - in' o - ver **home,**

home, **home.**

Develop an accompaniment of your own as suggested by the style here. Begin with the piano accompaniment which can be played on other percussion instruments. Chords may be played on autoharp, guitar, or banjo. Play a chord on the downbeat of each bar and/or a pattern similar to the right hand piano part.

The bass instruments may play the left hand piano part one octave higher than written. Ad-lib percussion parts using these or similar patterns:

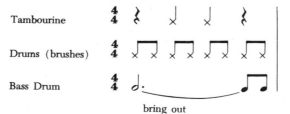

This descant may be played on harmonica, flute, or any other appropriate instrument. (Transpose one whole tone up for clarinet.) Play any phrase in any octave.

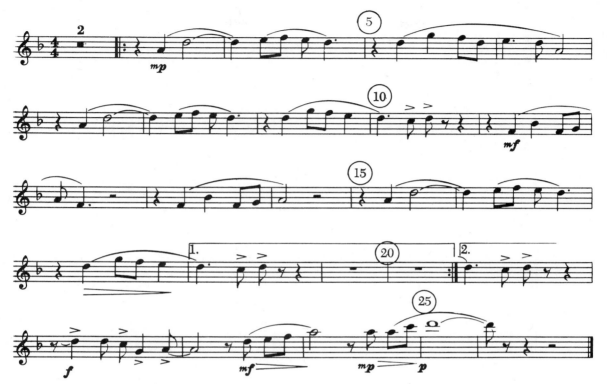

Wanderin'

American Folk Song
Adapted and Arr. B. A. R.

Here is another old song in "new dress."

I've been work-in' in the cit-y, I've been work-in' on the farm. But all I've got to show for it is mus-cle in my arm, And it looks like I'm nev-er gon-na cease my wan-der-in'.

*Gong, bell tree, or cymbal (glissando on bells will create bell-tree effect).

looks like   I'm   nev - er gon - na cease my   wan - der-

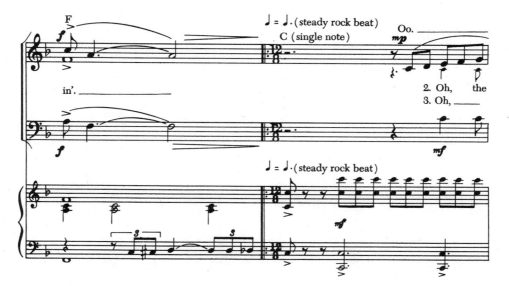

in'. _____

Oo. _____

2. Oh,   the
3. Oh, _____

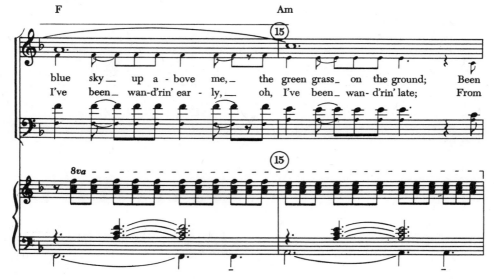

blue   sky_ up a - bove me,_ the green grass_ on the ground; Been
I've been_ wan-d'rin' ear - ly,_ oh, I've been_ wan- d'rin' late; From

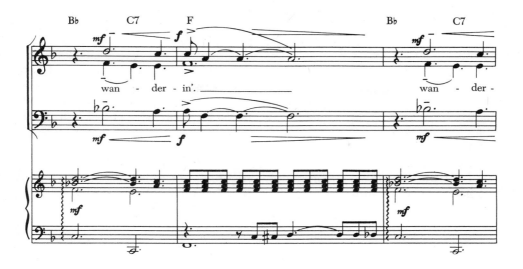

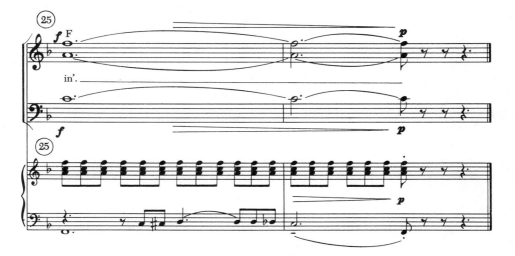

Develop your own accompaniment as suggested by the piano accompaniment printed here. Two piano players can play the part—one person playing the treble and another the bass. Autoharps and guitars may play the chords. Play the first section in a free manner following the vocal parts. In the $\frac{12}{8}$ section, play these rhythmic patterns.

Pastures of Plenty

by Woody Guthrie

Woody Guthrie spent most of his life drifting around the country, playing his guitar and singing his songs. As he roamed the country, he wrote more than a thousand songs reporting what he saw. Guthrie was born in 1912 and died in 1967, but he is very much a man of our time. He has been called the most gifted balladeer of this century. He was given honors for making Americans aware of their land and their heritage. He has been credited with touching off the revival of folk singing in the 50's and 60's. His fervent love of America was expressed in songs like "This Land Is Your Land." He gave a hopeful aura to the devastating Oklahoma dust-bowl years in "So Long," another folk classic. His son, Arlo Guthrie, is also a well-known singer. "Pastures of Plenty" is typical of Guthrie's folk collection. On your recording the song is sung by Lester Flatt with Earl Scruggs playing the banjo. Words of the song follow.

It's a mighty hard row that my poor hands have hoed,
My poor feet, I've traveled one hot dusty road.
Out of your dust bowl and westward we rolled
And your deserts was hot and your mountains was cold.

I've worked in your orchards of peaches and prunes,
I've slept on the ground in the light of your moon.
On the edge of the city you'll see us and then
We come with the dust and we go with the wind.

California, Arizona, we make all your crops.
Then it's up north to Oregon to gather your hops.
Take the beets from your ground, Take the grapes from your vine
To place on your table your light, sparkling wine.

Green pastures of plenty from dry desert ground,
From the Grand Coolee Dam where the waters run down
Every state in this union us migrants has been.
We've come with the dust and we're gone with the wind.

Well, it's always we rambled, this river and I,
All your green valleys I'll work 'til I die.
My land I'll defend with my life need it be
For my pastures of plenty must always be free.
Yes, my pastures of plenty must always be free.

I'm Gonna Be A Country Girl Again

Written and Sung by Buffy Sainte-Marie

Buffy Sainte-Marie was born a Cree Indian. Her songs include many in protest of the fate of the American Indian. She writes and sings in several styles and is one of the leading folk singers of today. This song in country style is her own song, but it also has features of folk music. Which features can you identify? In what ways does the style of singing seem appropriate to the style of the song?

He's Gone Away

American Folk Song

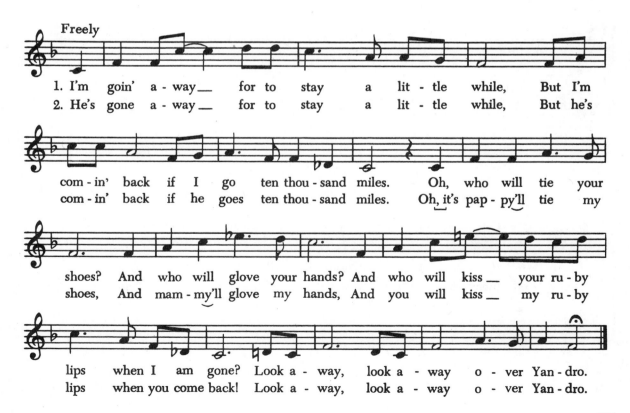

Freely

1. I'm goin' a-way___ for to stay a lit-tle while, But I'm
2. He's gone a-way___ for to stay a lit-tle while, But he's

com-in' back if I go ten thou-sand miles. Oh, who will tie your
com-in' back if he goes ten thou-sand miles. Oh, it's pap-py'll tie my

shoes? And who will glove your hands? And who will kiss___ your ru-by
shoes, And mam-my'll glove my hands, And you will kiss___ my ru-by

lips when I am gone? Look a-way, look a-way o-ver Yan-dro.
lips when you come back! Look a-way, look a-way o-ver Yan-dro.

Whoopee Ti-Yi-Yo

Cowboy Song
Arranged by Kurt Miller

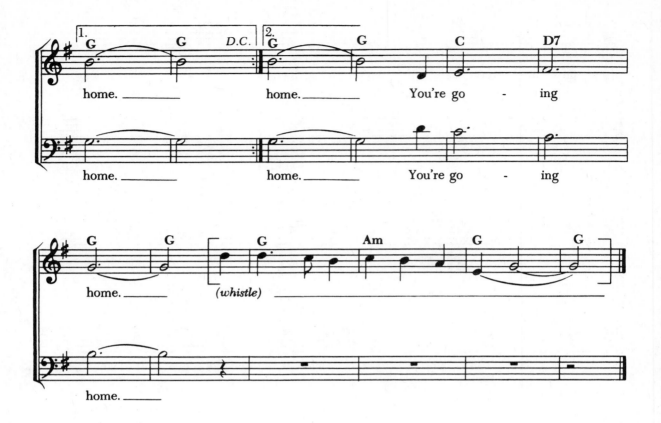

home. _____ home. _____ You're go - ing

home. _____ home. _____ You're go - ing

home. _____ (whistle) _____

home. _____

Develop an accompaniment to play on percussion instruments. Choose one or more of these patterns, or compose some of your own.

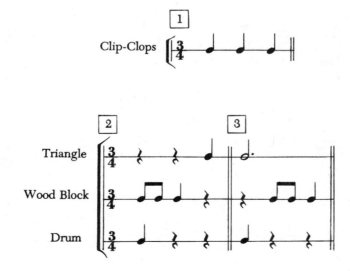

Clip-Clops

Triangle

Wood Block

Drum

Joy Is Like the Rain

Words and Music
by Sr. Miriam Therese, SCMM

1. I saw rain-drops on my win-dow, Joy _____ is like the
2. I saw clouds up-on a moun-tain, Joy _____ is like a
3. I saw rain-drops on the riv-er, Joy _____ is like the

rain. _____ Laugh-ter runs a-cross my pain, slips a-way and
cloud. _____ Some-times sil-ver, some-times grey, al-ways sun not
rain. _____ Bit by bit the riv-er grows, till all at once it

comes a-gain. Joy is like the rain. _____
far a-way. Joy is like a cloud. _____
o-ver-flows. Joy is like the rain. _____

The Power and Glory

Words and Music
by Phil Ochs
Arr. B. A. R.

charles ives
and
his music

Can you sing "America" in the key of E flat while someone plays the accompaniment in the key of C? As a boy, Charles Ives played this game with his father. He became accustomed to the tone color of many sounds occurring simultaneously. Later he composed music with the full spectrum of sound, finding it neither difficult or unusual, nor to be avoided. In one of his works, the orchestra imitates the sound of two marching bands playing different pieces as they come together in a parade. Sections of the orchestra are required to play in different keys and meters. The musical picture is very real. With great skill Ives was able to "tell it as it is" musically.

Charles Ives spent his life in Connecticut, where his parents and their families had lived from the earliest days of New England. Charles' father was an army band director during the Civil War and after that directed the community band in Danbury. Charles grew up hearing and liking the music of Beethoven and many other composers. He knew and liked the popular music of his own and his father's time—dance tunes, gospel hymns, marches, Civil War and patriotic songs. He loved such songs as "Turkey in the Straw," "Marching through Georgia," "America, the Beautiful," and his favorite, "Columbia, the Gem of the Ocean." These and similar melodies appear dozens of times in Ives' compositions, always freshened with new sounds of the composer.

A religious man and a lover of Americana, Ives believed musicians should "include the universe" and "use all the faculties the Creator has given man." Natural as his music sounded in his own mind, and natural as it sounds to many listeners nowadays, when written in notation for performers, it can look quite formidable. His music sometimes is conducted by two or three conductors at the same time, each indicating different rhythms and other musical content to different sections of the orchestra. One clever conductor learned to conduct a composition with three simultaneous rhythms by beating one with his right hand, one with his left, and nodding his head vigorously in the third.

The music of Ives was not appreciated by most people who heard it in his own time. Today we recognize it as the product of the fine and imaginative mind of a great American. Although he lived from 1874 to 1954, Charles Ives is truly a composer of your time.

Here are two of Charles Ives' favorite songs.

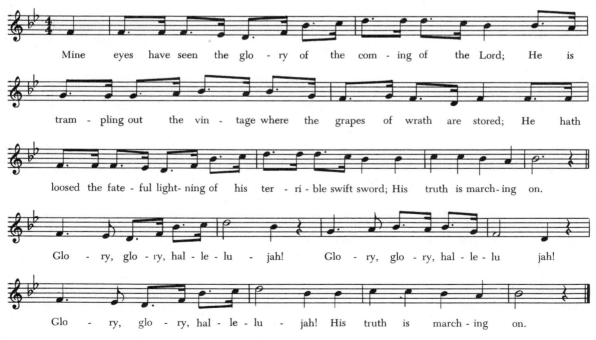

Mine eyes have seen the glo - ry of the com - ing of the Lord; He is tram - pling out the vin - tage where the grapes of wrath are stored; He hath loosed the fate - ful light- ning of his ter - ri - ble swift sword; His truth is march- ing on.

Glo - ry, glo - ry, hal - le - lu - jah! Glo - ry, glo - ry, hal - le - lu jah! Glo - ry, glo - ry, hal - le - lu - jah! His truth is march - ing on.

129

O Co - lum - bia, the gem of the o - cean, The home of the brave_ and the free,___

The shrine of each pa - triot's de - vo - tion, A world_of - fers hom - age to thee.

Thy__ man - dates make he - roes as - sem - ble, When Lib - er - ty's form_ stands in view;

Thy__ ban - ners make tyr - an - ny trem - ble, When_ borne_ by the red, white, and blue.

Refrain

When _ borne by the red, white, and blue, When _ borne by the red, white, and blue;

Thy__ ban - ners make tyr - an - ny trem - ble, When_ borne_ by the red, white, and blue.

Fourth of July

by Charles Ives

Charles Ives enjoyed national holidays, and he wrote a group of pieces called *A Symphony: Holidays* with titles "Washington's Birthday," "Decoration Day," "Fourth of July," and "Thanksgiving." In the preface of "Fourth of July" the composer wrote, "It's a boy's '4th' —no historical orations—no patriotic grandiloquences by 'grown-ups'—no program in his yard! But he knows what he's celebrating—better than some of the county politicians. And he goes at it in his own way, with a patriotism, nearer kin to nature than jingoism. His festivities start in the quiet of the midnight before and grow raucous with the sun. Everybody knows what it's like. The day ends with the skyrocket over the Church-steeple, just after the annual explosion sets the Town-Hall on fire."

When you have enjoyed the composition as a whole several times, listen especially for the passages in which the two melodies on this and the previous page are quoted. Describe Ives' use of them. What other "memorabilia" of the holiday can you hear? Listen for the build-up in the music, and describe the layers of sound you hear. What purpose is served by the quiet final passage? The climax, with the "annual explosion," is contained in two violent measures almost as loud as a sonic boom. But the following five measures, which describe the "skyrocket over the Church-steeple," are even more complex. This musical noise is made by thirteen different rhythm patterns played by winds and brasses, seven patterns in percussion, tone clusters on the piano, and twenty-four string parts with glissandos and different rhythms, all marked **ffff**. No wonder the performance often uses two conductors!

130

Shall We Gather at the River

Page from a hymnal with shape note notation

Sonata Number Four for Violin,

Third Movement

by Charles Ives (1874-1954, USA)

This movement is based on the hymn tune notated above, "Shall We Gather at the River." The piano accompaniment consists mainly of ninth chords which are harmonically independent of the violin melody. Besides the complete change in the accompaniment, what other alterations do you hear? Trace the melody as it appears throughout the violin part, and discover Ives' use of it. What are his methods of altering or retaining original passages from the hymn tune?

At a later time review the three instrumental compositions by Ives that you have studied, including "Variations on America," page 56. List and discuss the composer's musical preferences and the elements of his style which you could identify in these compositions.

Memories

Words and Music
by Charles Ives

We're sit-ting in the op-era house, the op-era house, the op-era house; We're wait-ing for the cur-tain to a-rise with won-ders for our eyes; We're feel-ing pret-ty gay, and well we may, "O, Jim-my, look!" I say, "The band is tun-ing up and soon will start to play." We whis-tle and we hum, _____ beat _____ time _____ with the drum.

(Whistle) _____ We whis-tle and we hum, _____ beat _____ time _____ with the drum, _____

(Whistle) _____ We're sit-ting in the

op - era house, the op - era house, the op - era house, a - wait - ing for the

cur - tain to ___ rise with won - ders for our eyes, a feel - ing of ex -

pec - tan - cy, a cer - tain kind of ec - sta - sy, ex - pec - tan - cy and

ec - sta - sy, ex - pec - tan - cy and ec - sta - sy ___ Sh'-s'-s'-s. ___ Curtain!

Adagio **_p_** **B**

From the street a strain ___ on my ear doth fall, A ___

tune as thread-bare as that "old red shawl." It is tat-tered, it is torn, It shows

signs of be - ing worn, It's the tune my Un-cle hummed from ear - ly morn. 'Twas a

com - mon lit - tle thing and kind 'a sweet, But 'twas sad and seemed to slow up both his

feet; I can see him shuf-fling down to the barn or to the town, A - -

hum - - - - - - - - - ming. ___

The Circus Band

Words and Music
by Charles Ives

have died? Can! that! rot! She ___ is pass-ing, but she

sees me not. ___

Where is ___ the la - dy all in pink? Last

year ___ she waved to me, I think; Can she ___ have died?

Can! that! rot! She ___ is pass - ing, but she sees me not!

Quotation from *Postface to 114 Songs*

by Charles Ives

*Some of the songs in this book, particularly among the later ones, cannot be sung, and if they could, perhaps might prefer, if they had a say, to remain as they are; that is, "in the leaf"—and that they will remain in this peaceful state is more than presumable. An excuse (if none of the above are good enough) for their existence which suggests itself at this point is that a song has a **few** rights, the same as other ordinary citizens. If it feels like walking along the left-hand side of the street, passing the door of physiology or sitting on the curb, why not let it? If it feels like kicking over an ash can, a poet's castle, or the prosodic law, will you stop it? Must it always be a polite triad, a "breve gaudium," a ribbon to match the voice? Should it not be free at times from the dominion of the thorax, the diaphragm, the ear, and other points of interest? If it wants to beat around in the valley, to throw stones up the pyramids, or to sleep in the park, should it not have some immunity from a Nemesis, a Rameses, or a policeman? Should it not have a chance to sing to itself, if it can sing?—to enjoy itself without making a bow, if it can't take a bow?—to swim around in any ocean, if it can swim, without having to swallow "hook and bait," or being sunk by an operatic greyhound? If it happens to feel like trying to fly where humans cannot fly, to sing what cannot be sung, to walk in a cave on all fours, or to tighten up its girth in blind hope and faith and try to scale mountains that are not, who shall stop it?*

    —In short, must a song
    always be a song!

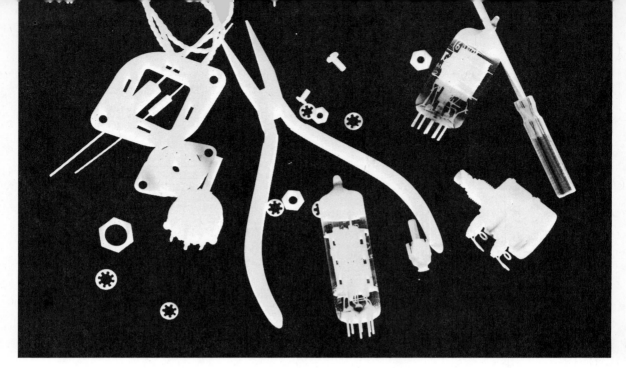

experiments in music II

Take some cues from Charles Ives and experiment with musical sounds.

1. Create new instruments that will produce unusual sounds. As a child, Ives explored musical sound by tuning bottles and glasses. He was able to play quarter tones as well as the twelve chromatic tones. Sometimes he played melodies written for the piano on one set of bottles or glasses and filled in with ornamental quarter-tone runs on another set. He also created new scales and composed melodies with these tones. Invent some tuned instrument of your own, and see what musical ideas you can derive from it.

2. Ives said that beauty in music is often confused with something that lets the ear lie back in an easy chair. His music surprises the listener and requires him to be alert and thoughtful. In creating new harmonies, Ives often added thirds above the usual chords. Work in twos. On the piano play the CEG chord, then add the 7th tone—B, then the 9th tone—D, the 11th tone—F, the 13th tone—A. Notice the change in the sound of the chord each time you add a tone. Experiment with these chords in different octaves and with the tones in different positions in the chord. Accompany a melody such as "Twinkle, Twinkle, Little Star" with some of these chords.

   Play tone clusters on the piano with your arm or a ruler. Try different dynamics and ranges. Play an accompaniment for some familiar melody with tone clusters.

3. Play polytonal harmony. While one person plays "America" in one key in the middle part of the piano, another might play it in a different key in the lower part of the piano. Explore various keys and ranges. Play polytonal

harmony by playing in canon. As one person plays "America" in the key of G, another might play it in the same key but begin at the second note, or the second measure, of the first performance. Try different time intervals for beginning the second part, and try different ranges of the piano.

4. Ives played around his father's band rehearsals from the time he could walk. He was accustomed to hearing the music from "close up" and "far away." Later in his compositions he planned unusual positions for members of the orchestra. Sometimes he imagined the brass group playing from the loft of the church; sometimes he asked the strings of the orchestra to sit in a different part of the concert hall from the rest of the orchestra. With players from your class, experiment with "stereo" sounds. Separate instrumental groups. Try different effects with the same sound, such as loud and far away, soft and near.

5. Work in a group of five. Select a few of your favorite songs. Choose phrases from them and devise clever ways of connecting them, singing them simultaneously, singing them in imitation or in any other way that seems effective. Create a new song from your materials.

6. Make instruments from plastic containers; for example, a soap bottle with rice inside. Prepare bleach bottles by putting beans inside and draping the outside with junk jewelry tied on fishline. Make bells from clay flower pots with rope holding the clappers. Make bongo drums by cutting the tops off large plastic containers and inserting forms of plywood or composition. A tin can struck at different points with a metal mallet will give different pitches. Discover other instruments you can quickly contrive.

Explore the sound possibilities and develop a vocabulary of sounds you will use in a composition. Write symbols for the sounds and complete your composition on paper. Then play it from the notation.

music from distant places

The great variety of the world's music is one of the most fascinating aspects of musical exploration. Each region develops musical features that seem to belong especially to that locale. The rhythms of Africa, music for the circle dances of Greece, the exotic melodies and rhythms of Asia all have qualities easily identified with the place of origin. The same elements of music constitute songs of the English countryside, Spain and Mexico, and Eastern Europe. Yet the variety we find in the arrangement of the elements and the strong regional character that results is astonishing. In this section of your book you will sing and listen to music with distinctive regional sounds. Review the basic elements of music on page 32, and discover the different changes in these elements that result in sounds of the regions represented. Discover the life style and events reflected in the music of different peoples.

Bwana, Ibariki Afrika

African Folk Song

This prayer is sung by many people in Africa. The Swahili words mean, "Bless O Lord, our country, Africa." The language is the most common African language. The words are pronounced phonetically. Listen to the recording of the song.

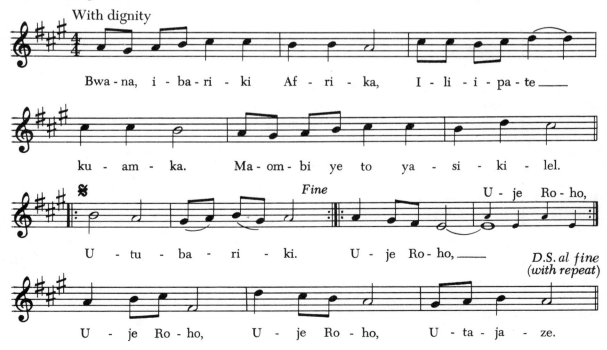

Musical Instruments in Africa

The music of Africa is as colorful as the vast continent itself. With dozens of large countries and scores of different native tribes, the continent is highly varied. Although African music reflects the character of the people as a whole, the music of each tribe reflects some features that are different. African music is closely related to the language. Since each tribe has its own language, this accounts for some of the unique musical qualities. The character of the place where the people live also affects the music, as instruments are made from materials close at hand. Some tribes play on drums of bark and cowhide, others on drums of clay and lizard skin. Flutes are played in areas where reeds and bamboo grow. On your recording are three examples of music played by people of different tribes on instruments they have constructed.

Nsiriba Ya Munange Katego

Entenga drums are played in the region of Kampala, Uganda. They are tuned, cone-shaped drums. This tune is played on fifteen tuned drums. Four men play on twelve drums which are tuned to two octaves of a pentatonic scale, and two men play three bass drums. The drum tune is taken from a folk song of the country.

Musingasinga Yakora Egali

The xylophones heard here are made by balancing large pieces of wood on two freshly-cut banana stalks. The pieces of wood are saved and new stalks cut each time the instrument is set up. With mallets the players beat the ends, not the middle, of the pieces of wood. If the pieces jump out of place, they are quickly replaced. On this recording, a group of men play for the Ntara dance on sixteen-tone xylophones.

Manyanda

A "singing gourd" is made by stretching a thin skin across one end of a gourd and making a hole in the pointed end through which the

player sings. The instrument is used as a trumpet for signals, and songs are played on it. The size of the gourd determines the pitch. The dance song from Zambia is played on singing gourds after an introduction of drumming and singing.

Harusi

Unlike other instruments, the "thumb piano" is found everywhere in Africa. It is known by dozens of different names in different languages. The instrument may have as many as thirty-six tones, but most have about a dozen. Metal or bamboo tongues are attached to a piece of wood by a metal bar. The free ends are plucked by the thumbs and forefingers. "Harusi" is a wedding tune played in Central Tanzania where the instrument is called the malimba mbira.

Sarakatsani Song

Greek Folk Song

The Sarakatsani are a nomadic tribe of Greek shepherds who roam the Middle East. This song and the next one are typical of folk songs from Greece. The dance rhythms and minor sound of Greek melodies are enjoyed everywhere. The $\frac{7}{8}$ meter is counted in three beats to the measure in this division: (3 + 2 + 2)

With spirit

Gm

BOYS:

1. & 2.
Choose, daugh - ter, choose, my dear, and __ name your wed - ding
Three faith - ful ones, my dear, a - wait to hear you

D7 [1.] [2.] D7 GIRLS: Gm

day; _____ say. _____ 1. O fa - ther, is he
2. O fa - ther, can he

Cm Gm D7 Gm

hand - some? O fa - ther, is he rich? _____ O
dance well? O fa - ther, can he sing? _____ O

Cm Gm D7 Gm

fa - ther, does he love me? __ Can you not tell me which? __
fa - ther, does he love me? __ Tell me the joy he'll bring! __

Accompany "Sarakatsani Song" by playing the chords on the autoharp and these percussion patterns on classroom instruments.

Finger cymbals

Tambourine — Repeat throughout

Drums HIGH LOW

141

Starlight Dance

Greek Folk Song
English words by B. L.
Arr. by B. A. R.

Greek people often express their moods and feelings in dance. This is one of the circle dances in which the Greeks move with small steps around the circle holding hands at shoulder height. Play a percussion accompaniment with these patterns.

To dance, to dance and laugh and sing, Sing and laugh and

dance and sing, To dance and sing. The hours, the hours of

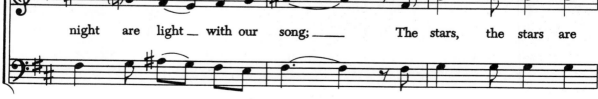

night are light with our song; The stars, the stars are

bright to dance_ and_ sing_ and laugh_ and_ dance. Eh - yah -

1. 2.

ee yah- eh_ yah - ee, Eh - yah - ee yah- eh_ yah - ee, Eh - yah - ee.

Nisiōtikōs Choros (Island Dance)

The **bouzoukee** is a string instrument of Greece that looks somewhat like a mandolin and is played with a plectrum. Music played on the instrument also is called "bouzoukee." It is the most popular music in restaurants and places of entertainment in Greece. The *syrtos* is an ancient shuffling circle dance with a leader. The leader may do leaps and acrobatic figures around the inside of the circle while the circle continues to move counterclockwise with small steps. On the recording the *syrtos* is played on a bouzoukee accompanied by drums and string bass.

143

Landlord

Steel Band Music from Trinidad

Calypso rhythms of the island of Trinidad in the Caribbean are a special sound in Western music. Calypso music is sung, and its rhythms are played on percussion instruments, many of which have been invented by the people of Trinidad. The large oil industry of the island provides steel barrels and from these the famous steel bands have developed. By experimenting, people noticed that dents in the barrels resulted in different pitches. Later, the instrument was refined by cutting off the top end of the barrel, heating the lower end, and hammering out separate dents of different sizes and shapes. A kind of tuned gong resulted. The beaters usually are sticks wrapped in strips of rubber. The only non-metal instrument in the steel band is the shac-shac — a gourd filled with seeds. "Landlord" is a typical steel band performance from Trinidad. Notice the calypso rhythms.

Sounds from the Far East

The musical sounds developed by man are of astonishing number and variety. Music produced by the human voice and on instruments reflects much of the culture of each ethnic group around the world. Primitive and sophisticated civilizations of the past and of the present can be identified through music which is unique to each of them.

Listen to three types of music from three places in the East. Discover the charm and means of expression of each.

Dhun

This music from India is played on a double drum and three instruments called sahnai. The sahnai are oboe-like instruments that have been common in India for thousands of years. A long reed gives it the special tone quality. In the music one of the sahnai plays a one-tone drone. The others play an ornamented version of a folk tune in Dorian mode.

Echigoshi

This folk song is based on a dance performed in the festivals of Echigo in eastern Japan. It is played on the koto, the most common traditional Japanese instrument. About six feet long, the koto has thirteen silk strings which the performer plucks or strums with ivory picks attached to his fingers.

The music begins slowly with only the single notes of the melody played simply. Gradually the tempo quickens, and many ornaments and embellishments are added.

Ketjak Chorus

On the island of Bali, after dark, the village men sit in close circles shouting sounds that enhance a story told by two actors. The story concerns an army of monkeys, and the voices are imitating the imagined sounds. For this reason, the shouting is called Ketjak or "monkey" chorus. Percussion instruments set the tempo and add other rhythms. The women standing at the edge of the circle repeat a wailing refrain.

Scarborough Fair

English Folk Song
Arranged by Fred Bock

Warmly and freely

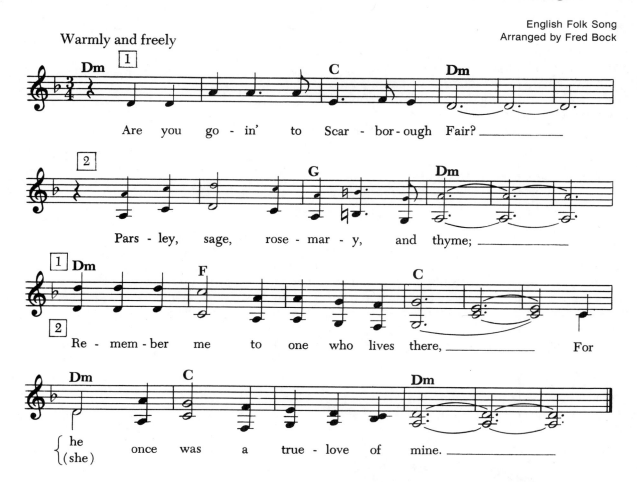

Are you go - in' to Scar - bor - ough Fair? _____

Pars - ley, sage, rose - mar - y, and thyme; _____

Re - mem - ber me to one who lives there, _____ For

{ he
(she) } once was a true - love of mine. _____

This folk song has been sung for generations in England and the United States. Recently it has been a popular choice of pop-folk singers. The simpler version given first is much like the original folk song. Play the autoharp in the style of the lute. Add the bell part and play finger cymbals in any pattern you choose, or improvise as you play.

2   For { he / (she) } once was a true-love of mine, —

For she once was { a / a } true-love of mine, ____

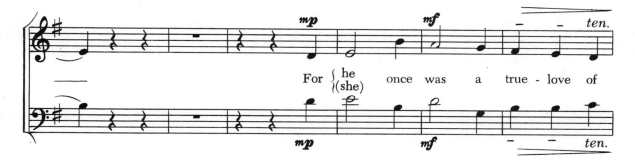

For { he / (she) } once was a true-love of

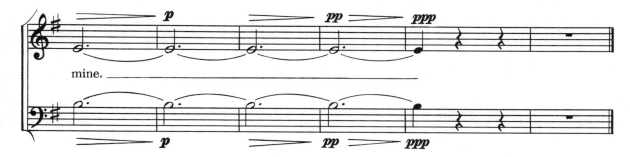

mine. ____

Henry Martin

Old English Ballad

1. There were ____ three broth - ers in mer - ry Scot - land, In
2. The lot ____ it fell up - on Hen - ry Mar - tin, The
3. He had not been sail - ing but a long win - ter's night, And
4. "Hel - lo, ____ hel - lo," ____ cried Hen - ry Mar - tin, "What

mer - ry Scot - land there were three, _____ And they did cast
young - est of all ____ the three, _____ That he should turn
part of a short win - ter's day, _____ Be - fore he es -
makes ____ you sail ____ so nigh?" ____ "I'm a rich mer - chant

lots which of them ____ should go, ____ should go, ____ should
rob - ber on all the salt sea, ____ salt sea, ____ salt
pied a stout lof - ty ship, ____ a ship, ____ a
ship bound for fair Lon - don town, ____ fair Lon - don

go _____ And ____ turn rob - ber all on the salt sea. _____
sea _____ For to main - tain his two broth - ers and he. _____
ship _____ Come ____ a - rid - ing down on him straight-way. _____
town, _____ Will ____ you please for to let me pass by?" _____

5. "Oh, no, oh, no," cried Henry Martin,
"That thing it never can be,
For I have turned robber on all the salt sea, salt sea, salt sea
For to maintain my two brothers and me.

6. "Then lower your topsail and bow down your mizzen,
Bow yourselves under my lee,
Or I shall give you a fast-flowing ball, a fast-flowing ball
And cast your dear bodies down in the salt sea."

7. With broadside and broadside and at it they went,
   For fully two hours or three,
   Till Henry Martin give to her the death shot, the death shot, the death shot
   And straight to the bottom went she.

8. Bad news, bad news to old England came,
   Bad news to old London town,
   There's been a rich vessel and she's cast away, away, away
   And all of her merry men drowned.

La madrugada

Spanish Folk Song

Ma - dru - ga - da ye - ra la u - na, que ni
u - na, ni me - di a, ni na - da, Co - mo la ma - dru -
ga - da, a la di - a - na.

Repeat this for additional lyrics in other stanzas.

2. Madrugada y eran las dos,
   que ni dos, ni una, ni media, ni nada.
   Como la madrugada, a la diana.

3. Madrugada y eran las tres,
   que ni tres, ni dos, ni una, ni media, ni nada.
   Como la madrugada, a la diana.

4. Madrugada y eran las cuatro,
   que ni cuatro, ni tres, ni dos, ni una, ni media, ni nada.
   Como la madrugada, a la diana.

To suggest the gong of a large clock, play this piano part on the downbeat of each measure.

Play a chime or bell on each number.

151

El son del viento (Sound of the Wind)

Mexican Folk Melody

This folk melody from the state of Michoacan in Mexico is played on the harp. This folk type of harp is heard in village market places and plazas where people passing by may give coins to the player. In this part of Mexico the rich culture of mixed Spanish, Indian, and Black heritage has resulted in very interesting folk music.

A la capotín

(The Cape)

Spanish Folk Song

Yo soy fir - me ___ pa - ra a - mar - te ___ y cons - tan - te en el que-
rer. ___ Que tra - ba - jos ___ pa - sa un hom - bre ___ cuan - do
quie - re a un - a mu - jer. ___ Yo soy jer. ___ A la ca - po-
tín - tín - tín - tín es - ta no - che va llo - ver. ___ A la ca - po-
tín - tín - tín - tín que se - rá la ma - ne - cer. ___ A la ca - po-

tín - tín - tín - tín es - ta no - che va llo - ver.____ A la ca - po -

tín - tín - tín - tín que se - rá la ma - ne - cer.____

Make up a percussion accompaniment using these patterns.

Tambourine

Castanets

Guantanamera
(Lady of Guantanamo)

Spanish words by José Marti

The entire song is based on this chord progression:

Guitar and autoharp players may make up patterns such as these:

The root notes of the chord progression make a bass line.

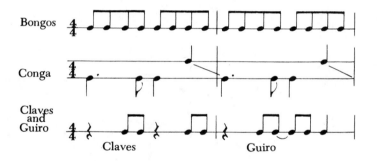

Make up patterns with percussion instruments.

A few voices may sing this vocal ostinato during all or part of the song.

Vocal Ostinato

Guan - ta - na - mer- a

The literal translation of the Spanish is as follows:

I'm a sincere man from the land of palms. Before dying, I wish to pour forth the poems of my soul.

My verses are soft green but also a flaming red. My verses are like wounded fauns seeking refuge in the forest.

I want to share my fate with the world's humble. A little mountain stream pleases me more than the ocean.

Der Bergwalzer

German Folk Song
Arranged by Kurt Miller

1. Wie könn - te denn heu - te die
2. Der Land-mann der könn - te den
3. Der Mül - ler, der könn - te das

Welt noch be - ste - hen, wenn
Ak - ker nicht bau - en, wenn } kei - ne Berg - leut' wär'n, Glück auf! 's kommt
Korn nicht ver - mah - len, wenn

Noch ein - mal, ja, ja,
al - les von' Berg - leut' her! _____ noch ein - mal, noch ein - mal,

ja, ja, 's kommt al - les von' Berg - leut' her! _____
noch ein - mal, noch ein - mal, al - les von' Berg - leut' her, Glück auf!

Der Bergwalzer

Songs of the Don Cossacks

Choral groups from different countries and times employ different styles of singing appropriate to the songs they sing. One would expect the robust style you hear in the recording of these Russian folk songs. The Cossacks were military horsemen in Russia before 1917. The Don Cossacks chorus was originally made up of former Cossack officers. The chorus became well-known throughout the world. Members changed from time to time, and eventually all members of the chorus became citizens of the United States. The style of their singing is unique and especially appropriate for the folk songs of their repertoire. Listen to the songs sung in Russian, and notice the choral style.

Russian Song

This is a jeering song. Some boys seem to be making fun of the old grandpa of the village. They describe him, saying that a crow has built a nest in his old fur cap and has laid eggs there! And there's a bee in his beard!

Is it true? Yes, true!
His old shoes with wooden nails
Really look like wooden pails!
Is it true? Yes, true!
And in his shaggy beard lives a bumble bee!
Is it true? Yes, true!

The Golden Bee

Tell me, little golden bee,
Why are you humming?
Have you seen the lovely maid
Whose lips are red as roses
And as sweet as nectar?

157

patterns and designs in music: ostinato

A repeated note group called **ostinato** appears often in music. The term is an Italian word meaning "obstinate" or "persistent." An ostinato may be a melodic pattern, or it may be rhythmic only. It is featured as a persistent accompaniment to other musical material.

Review *Boléro* (page 104), and hear the composition described below. In both, the ostinato continues throughout. Ostinato patterns used less dramatically are very common. To learn something of the possibilities of this musical device, complete the following explorations.

1. Playing resonator bells, temple blocks, xylophone, or the piano, select an ostinato pattern from the pentatonic scale (the five tones of the black keys or a similar tone arrangement). While one person plays the ostinato repeatedly, take turns improvising melodic patterns against it. (Use the tones of the pentatonic scale in your melodies, also.)

2. Develop an ostinato with spoken words. Choose a few words that have a dramatic effect. Speak them dramatically, emphasizing the consonants or vowels or both. Experiment by using them in different ways: speak them in a whisper; speak them in harmony with several natural tone qualities; speak them with the accompaniment of one or more percussion instruments. When you have a variety of spoken ostinatos, improvise melodies with them. Use any of the twelve chromatic tones. Play a flute, clarinet, or other orchestral instrument; play the bells, piano, or any melody instrument available. Or sing melodies on a neutral syllable or with a text.

3. Develop ostinato patterns with percussion instruments or some unusual sound-makers you select. Improvise melodies or other rhythms against your percussion ostinatos.

Carmina Burana, Introduction, First Part

by Carl Orff (1895-   , Germany)

A brief introduction opens the dramatic cantata based on ancient "Songs of Beuren" from which it gets its title. The work is for solo singers, chorus, orchestra, and a large group of extra percussion including two pianos and five timpani. The introduction is an invocation to Fortune, Empress of the World. The general meaning of the Latin text is "Weep with me, all ye people, for fate crushes us." How does the rapid ostinato support the impassioned protest of the chorus? What is your opinion concerning the effectiveness of this accompaniment?

broadway musicals and movie music

The Sound of Music

The Sound of Music is one of the most popular musicals ever presented on stage and screen. It drew large audiences on Broadway and in movie theaters for ten years. It has been performed by numerous community, college, and high school casts.

Richard Rodgers composed the music, and Oscar Hammerstein wrote the lyrics. The two have collaborated on many other successful musicals including *Oklahoma!*, *Carousel*, *The King and I*, and *South Pacific*.

The story of *The Sound of Music* is based on the true story of the Trapp family, as described by Maria Trapp in her book, *The Trapp Family Singers*. The musical begins when Maria, a young postulant in an Austrian convent, is sent to the family of Captain van Trapp as governess of his seven children. The story then relates the developments of her life with the family to the time when she becomes wife and welcome stepmother. Her sincerity and charm win the children, and they soon grow to love her. She teaches them to sing so well that eventually the whole family is heard in concerts.

Singing as well as clever planning save them from being captured by the Nazis. At a folk song festival, they leave the concert stage one by one during their exit song and disappear to finally reach freedom on Maria's beloved mountain. Five well-known songs from the musical are sung on your recording. Listen to them, or have a Sing-Along.

Who Will Buy?

from *Oliver*

Words and Music
by Lionel Bart

Brightly (in 2)

Who will buy this won-der-ful morn - ing? Such a sky you

nev - er did see. ___ Who will tie it up with a rib-

bon, And put it in a box for me? ___ { So I can
There'll nev - er

see it at my lei - sure ___ When-ev - er things go wrong,___
be a day so sun - ny; ___ It could not hap - pen twice.__

And I would keep it as a trea - sure ___ To last my
Where is the man with all the mon - ey? ___ It's cheap at

whole life long.___ }
half the price! ___ } Who will buy this won-der-ful feel-

- ing? I'm so high, I swear I could fly. ___ Me, oh,

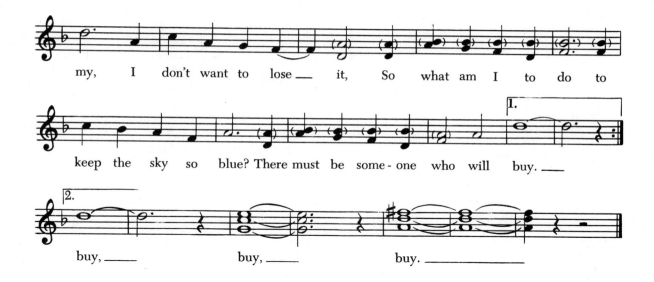

my, I don't want to lose — it, So what am I to do to

keep the sky so blue? There must be some-one who will buy. —

buy, — buy, — buy. —

Shalom

from *Milk and Honey*

Words and Music
by Jerry Herman
Arr. B. A. R.

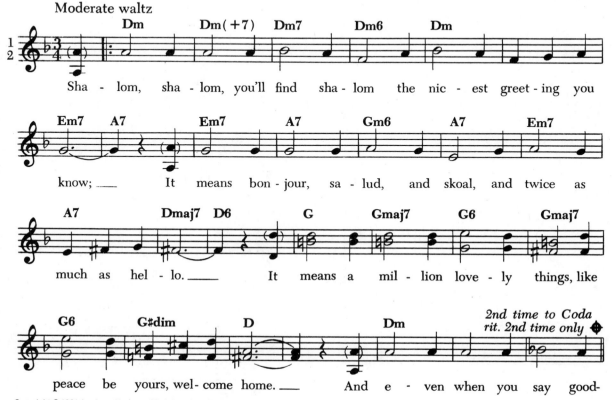

Sha - lom, sha - lom, you'll find sha - lom the nic - est greet - ing you

know; — It means bon - jour, sa - lud, and skoal, and twice as

much as hel - lo. — It means a mil - lion love - ly things, like

peace be yours, wel - come home. — And e - ven when you say good-

bye, you say good - bye with sha - lom. _____

Slowly and freely

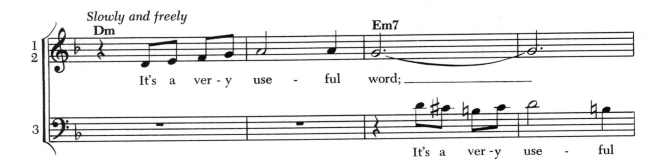

It's a ver - y use - ful word; _____

It's a ver - y use - ful

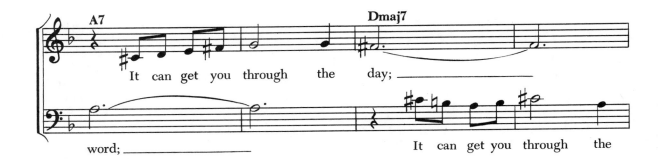

It can get you through the day; _____

word; _____

It can get you through the

All you real - ly need to know; ___ You can hard - ly go

day;

All you need to know; ___

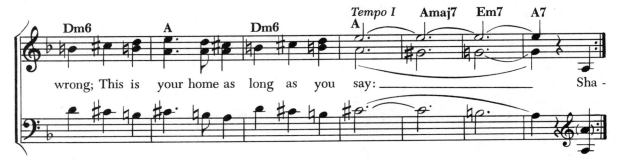

wrong; This is your home as long as you say: _____ Sha -

bye, If your voice has "I don't want to go" in it, Say good-bye with a

lit - tle "hel - lo" in it, And say good - bye with Sha - lom. _____

Here is an accompaniment for any appropriate melody instrument and per-cussion.

What's New Pussycat?

from *What's New Pussycat?*

Music by Burt Bacharach
Words by Hal David
Arr. B. A. R.

Perform this as a novelty song with humor. Create an "oom-pah-pah" feeling in this manner.

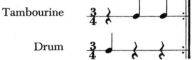

Play bells on all the "whoa" themes.

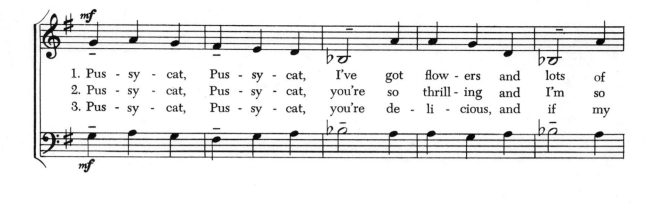

1. Pus - sy - cat, Pus - sy - cat, I've got flow-ers and lots of
2. Pus - sy - cat, Pus - sy - cat, you're so thrill - ing and I'm so
3. Pus - sy - cat, Pus - sy - cat, you're de - li - cious, and if my

hours ___ to spend with you, So go and pow - der your
will - ing to care for you, So go and make up your
wish - es can all come true, I'll soon be kiss - ing your

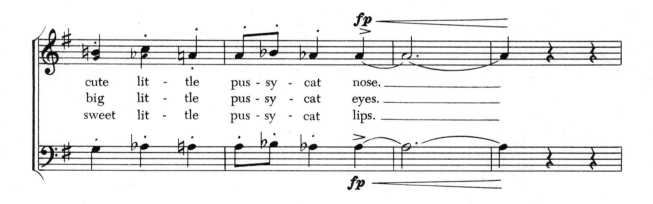

cute lit - tle pus - sy - cat nose. ___
big lit - tle pus - sy - cat eyes. ___
sweet lit - tle pus - sy - cat lips. ___

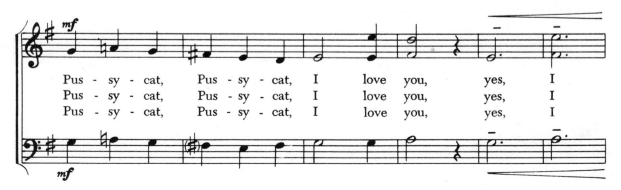

Pus - sy - cat, Pus - sy - cat, I love you, yes, I
Pus - sy - cat, Pus - sy - cat, I love you, yes, I
Pus - sy - cat, Pus - sy - cat, I love you, yes, I

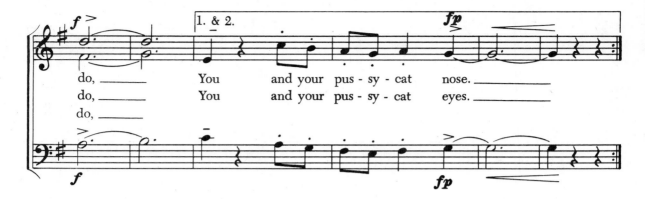

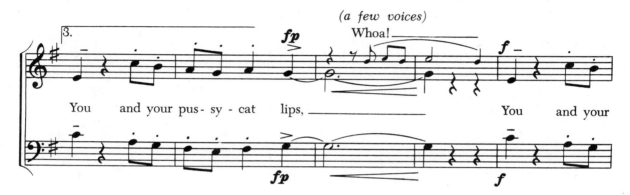

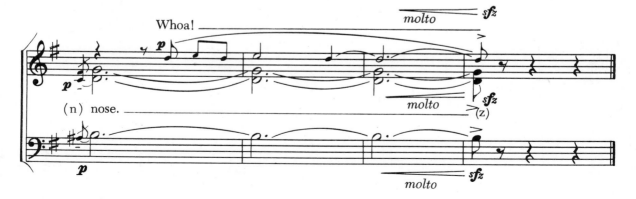

experiments in music III

Experiment with original music of your own and with notation for it. Complete one or more of the explorations described below. Tape your compositions so that you can review and discuss them later in class.

1. Work in a group of ten. Compose with spoken words only. Use the lines below, find a poem or quotation, or create your own lines. Experiment with the words and your voices. Develop pitch levels, rhythm, texture, tone qualities, dynamics, and organization that please you.

Fog

by Carl Sandburg

The fog comes
on little cat feet.

It sits looking
over harbor and city
on silent haunches
and then moves on.

From CHICAGO POEMS by Carl Sandburg. Copyright 1916 by Holt, Rinehart and Winston, Inc. Copyright 1944 by Carl Sandburg. Reprinted by permission of Holt, Rinehart and Winston, Inc.

The Hunter

by Ogden Nash

The hunter crouches in his blind
'Neath camouflage of every kind,
And conjures up a quacking noise
To lend allure to his decoys.
This grown-up man, with pluck and luck
Is hoping to outwit a duck.

Copyright 1949 by Ogden Nash. Reprinted by permission of Little, Brown and Company, and Curtis Brown, Ltd.

What a wonderful
day! No one in the village
doing anything.
—Haiku by Shiki

From CRICKET SONGS: JAPANESE HAIKU, translated and copyrighted © 1964 by Harry Behn. Reprinted by permission of Harcourt Brace Jovanovich, Inc., and Curtis Brown, Ltd.

2. Work in a group of five. Combine words, other sounds you can make with your voice, and snatches of songs. Create a composition which can be given one of these titles or a title of your own invention: "Summer Happening," "The Famous Five," "Happy Birthday!" "It's Christmas!"

Invent symbols for the sounds you used, and write notation for your composition. Invite another group to perform your composition from the notation.

patterns and designs in music: the rondo

The rondo is a simple plan for organizing musical material. One section returns regularly either in exact repetitions or in variations. The "episode" sections between may be different from each other as well as from the repeated section, resulting in a design such as A B A C A D A. To become acquainted with the rondo design, complete the explorations below and study the three compositions which follow.

1. As a class project, create a rondo in sounds without instruments. Chant this couplet, a motto of David Crockett, until you can say it rhythmically in unison.

I leave this rule for oth - ers when I'm dead:

Be al - ways sure you're right, then go a - head.

Clap the rhythm of the rhyme without saying the words aloud. Let this be the A section of your rondo. Think of other sounds you can make by tapping, stamping, rapping, jingling something, and so on. Take turns creating a new rhythm of the same length as A with different sound-makers. When you have found several interesting patterns, choose a few for the episode sections of your rondo. With clapping and your sound-makers, perform an entire rondo in this design: A B A C A D A.

With the same rhythm patterns, perform your rondo on percussion instruments.

With the same rhythms and any melodies you choose, perform the rondo on melodic instruments. Combine the three types of sounds imaginatively, and play the rondo with all members of the class participating.

The returning sections of a rondo may be somewhat varied. Create a variation on the A section of your rondo calling it A$_1$. Perform the rondo in this design: A A$_1$ B A$_1$ C A D A A$_1$.

2. Create a rondo with words and word sounds only. Begin with this verse:

"Sing me a song of a lad that is gone,
Say, could that lad be I?
Merry of soul he sailed on a day
Over the sea to Skye."

Decide on the design of your rondo. Make up some verses of your own. Make your verses humorous or exciting or in some way interesting in sound. Read your word rondo as choral verse. Use solos, groups, and chorus, and read with expression.

3. Create a rondo in dance. As you speak the verses, move around the room, each one creating his own movement. When you have some good ideas, dance the entire rondo with solos, groups, and chorus. Play a percussion instrument, snap your fingers, or clap while you move and speak.

Rondo for Bassoon and Orchestra

by Carl Maria von Weber (1786-1826, Germany)

Listen to the rondo by a German composer of a century and a half ago. Notice the tone color, range, and flexibility of the bassoon. Follow the rondo design. Notice the difference in the length of the sections.

A   Bassoon (string accompaniment)

A   Orchestra (oboe on melody at beginning)

B   Bassoon (French horns in introduction and accompaniment)

A_1 Orchestra (new ending)

C   Bassoon (strings prominent in accompaniment)

A   Bassoon

D   Bassoon (orchestral introduction based on B, oboe countermelody later)

Bridge Orchestra (based on A)

A   Bassoon

Coda   Orchestra and bassoon (orchestral accompaniment based on A against cadenzas of bassoon)

Rondo

from *Persian Set*

by Henry Cowell (1897-1965)

This composition is the result of an American composer's interest in the music of other lands. Henry Cowell lived for several months in Teheran where he listened to the music of Iran, a region formerly called Persia. He was especially fascinated by the music of small ensembles which include a drum, a three-string plucked instrument, wind instruments, and sometimes a singer. The composition was inspired by this experience. On your recording it is performed by small orchestra, mandolin, and men's voices. Listen to the fourth movement, "Rondo," of *Persian Set* and discover how the composer achieved the impression of Persian music. Discover the musical ideas that are Western.

There are nine sections in the rondo design, and they can be indicated with letters A to E. Write the outline with those letters. Fill in the first section in this way: A—a b a_1. Fill in the last section A—a b a_1 c a_2. Discover the meaning of these symbols, and fill in the other A sections as you listen again. Indicate the sounds featured in each episode section to complete your analysis outline.

Swingin' Round

from *The Riddle*

Played by The Dave Brubeck Quartet

One recent style of jazz combines musical ideas from the stream of improvisational jazz with sounds from classical music, resulting in "Third Stream." In Third Stream jazz, instruments often are played with techniques used by symphony players. Instruments such as the flute, cello, bassoon, or French horn, not formerly heard in jazz groups, may be added. Designs such as theme and variations or rondo, used by composers of formal music, may be borrowed.

In the Third Stream jazz performance called *The Riddle*, the players play variations for forty-five minutes on the English round, "Hey, Ho! Anybody Home?" Three musical sources

are skillfully used—the folk melody, jazz improvisation, and ideas borrowed from composed music. Review the folk melody below. Listen to the excerpt from *The Riddle*, and write the rondo design with letters of the alphabet. There are seven sections. Which sections are formal and which are "free"? How are the four instruments of the quartet used in each section?

Complete a class analysis of this rondo. On the blackboard write the letters which represent the sections in a column. Across the board, write the six elements and qualities of music (see page 32). Talk about each section and fill in your analysis.

Hey, Ho! Anybody Home?

English Round

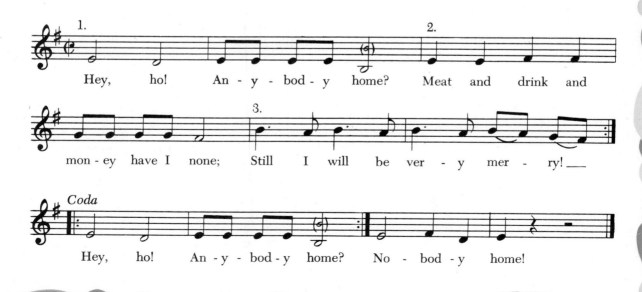

Hey, ho! An-y-bod-y home? Meat and drink and mon-ey have I none; Still I will be ver-y mer-ry!

Coda

Hey, ho! An-y-bod-y home? No-bod-y home!

Of Wood and Brass

by Vladimir Ussachevsky (1911-   , Russia, USA)

This work, composed in 1965, was named for the materials of the instruments played in the composition. The original sounds were played on trombone, trumpet, xylophone, and Korean gong. These were changed by manipulating the sounds on tape and running the tape recorder at several speeds. The composer said he tried to change the sounds as much as possible from the original instrumental sounds. Some purely electronic sounds were added.

The work is in four sections. The first consists primarily of sounds from a trombone, though some sounds from all other sources except trumpet also are heard. The second section is made from one single flourish on the trumpet. Most sounds of the third section were played originally on a xylophone. Electronic sounds are added. The last section is composed of one glissando on the trombone and the sound of a Korean gong.

When you have studied "Of Wood and Brass," read "Experiments in Music IV" in preparation for your own explorations with electronic sounds, and listen to the individual transformations of the sounds in "Of Wood and Brass" as they were developed.

Dripsody,

An Etude for Variable Speed Recorder

by Hugh Le Caine (1914-   , Canada)

This composition was derived from the sound of a single drop of water dripping from a faucet. The original tape recording of the sound was less then one-half inch long. This was copied on other tapes at various speeds to produce sounds with frequencies from 45 cycles per second to 8000 CPS. From these the composer selected sections of tape with the desired rhythmic patterns and spliced them together. These were combined in different ways as the sounds were re-recorded. Then the first sound was combined in different ways as the sounds were re-recorded. The first sound you hear is the original recording before any alteration.

experiments in music IV

Mr. Ussachevsky was asked to suggest ways in which you might experiment with electronic composition. Following are his suggestions. The examples Mr. Ussachevsky refers to are on your recording. Most of the examples are from "Of Wood and Brass." Of the more than forty tapes Mr. Ussachevsky made in working on that composition, he has extracted a few examples that illustrate the technical and creative processes involved.

Today electronic music is often heard on records, radio, and TV. It is used to accompany ballet. A surprising number of composers have written for musical instruments in combination with electronic sound. Popular music uses some simple electronic devices to produce special effects on musical instruments. Some electronic music today is produced on synthesizer and computer, but a good deal of it is the result of the well-established techniques of sound recording and sound manipulation with such devices as tape recorders, filters, ring-modulators, and echo devices. If some of these devices are available to you, create electronic music of your own.

A. Record various sounds that you happen to like, including those of musical instruments. You can record single sounds, machine or nature sounds, scales, melodies, chords, or numerous others. It is a good idea to record these sounds at two or three different speeds. This will constitute your "sound bank" or raw material.

B. You can transpose these sounds, that is play them twice or four times as fast or as slow, if you have a tape recorder with two or three speeds. This will make the sounds higher and shorter, or lower and longer. Note that the quality of sound is affected as well as the pitch. (Listen to Band 1 on the record.)

C. You can play the sounds backward at different speeds.

D. If you have a machine with a separate playback head, you can also prolong sounds as you record them by using a method of an "electronic feedback." You probably have heard "feedback" sound on TV. It is an automatically repeated sound or sound pattern made when the sound goes back and forth between the record and playback heads of a tape recorder. The sound can be made to repeat only a few times, or indefinitely. Listen to Band 2 of the recording for this effect.

E. On some stereo tape recorders you can produce "sound-on-sound;" that is, several layers of sound can be recorded on top of each other. This will be easier with two recorders.

In using two tape recorders, you may wish to transform your sounds further by using speed variation on the tape recorder from which you play or by additional prolongation of the sounds on the tape recorder on which you record.

With your experimental sounds you can begin composing. Follow some of these plans:

A. Cut your tapes in whatever segments you decide, and splice the segments together into longer patterns.

B. Plan how to combine these patterns. The simple "sound-to-sound" splicing of tape probably will produce interesting results. Combination of the patterns by re-recording them on top of each other will result in other sounds.

C. Using a stereo tape recorder, copy one of your already evolved sound patterns on the first track. Record another prepared sound pattern on the second track. Now listen to both together. This will teach you many things. If you have not already done so, the next time you can plan how to distribute various sounds on each of the tracks so that when combined they sound more interesting than singly.

D. By using the stereo mixing control you can get antiphonal effects. By rotating the mixing control you can move the sound back and forth across the channels to create an illusion of different directions.

E. If you have three tape recorders, you may wish to build a mixing panel. This will make it possible for the patterns you created and preserved on tape to be played on two tape recorders and combined on the third. You will learn how to balance the various tapes you are mixing, and you will learn how to synchronize two of your tape recorders so that the patterns you carefully prepared will fall together exactly as you planned. But you should continue to experiment, for sometimes accidental mixtures obtained by random combinations of patterns produce delightful surprises and give you fresh ideas.

In addition to tape recorders, microphones, feedback possibilities, and speed variations, there are many other ways to develop sound materials for electronic music. The additional equipment required is divided basically into two categories—sound generators and sound modifiers. All of these usually are found in synthesizers, but some can be obtained separately.

Band-pass filter This device subtracts or removes part of the sound, either the low or the high part of any sound, or both simultaneously. Thus the sound loses some of its character. Listen to Band 3a, b, c; it gives you three sounds in succession—the original sound, the same sound with the top overtones suppressed by a low-pass filter, and another with the bottom suppressed by a high-pass filter.

Ring-Modulator This device doubles, upward and downward, the entire content of each sound that passes through it, while, ideally, suppressing the original sound altogether. The ring-modulator requires that a sine-wave oscillator be used with it. By shifting the sine tone up and down the frequency scale, the timbre of sound fed into the ring-modulator is changed, sometimes with remarkable effect. On the synthesizers this shifting can be done by playing discreet sine tones on the keyboard, and feeding these tones into a ring-modulator.

Listen to Bands 4a, b, c, d, and e, which illustrate in sequence:

a. A note played on trombone as it sounds through the ring-modulator.

b. The same note thus changed played an octave lower.

c. A *portamento* or a glide on trombone played through ring-modulator.

d. An excerpt from the end of the composition "Of Wood and Brass" made entirely of several ring-modulated trombone glides.

e. A shifting of the note from example "a" above by means of the synthesizer keyboard.

Reverberation is one of the oldest ways to give music special effect. In electronic music special devices are used to add color to sounds, to prolong them, to conceal imperfect joining of spliced sounds, and to create an illusion of space and distance. Listen to Band 5 which has two sounds in succession; one is simply reverberated; the other has reverberations hanging on the second track after the original sound died out. (The original sound was that of the Korean gong, put through a ring-modulator.)

If you have access to a synthesizer, keep in mind that it can produce a great variety of sound and sound patterns, all of them electronically generated. All the modification processes described above can be applied to synthesizer-derived material. Even an average size synthesizer will give you band-pass filter, ring-modulator, and reverberation devices, as well as a keyboard, or comparable touch-sensitive device. It will even automatically produce sound sequences for you. But whether you have simple or complex equipment, the most important thing is using it effectively to combine the sound materials into imaginative compositions.

sounds and photo
study of dance

Dance, the oldest of the arts, has been a leading form of expression since man first imitated the ceremonious movements of birds. There is an infinite variety of types of dance, from that of primitive peoples in the interior of South America, Australia, Africa, and other places, to the most sophisticated types of stage dance.

Numerous forms of dance can be seen today in performances on stage and TV. Among the most popular of these is ballet. In the French courts during the seventeenth century, a language of movement was formalized with special positions for hands and feet, and traditions of choreography began to develop. These were standard for three hundred years. In the twentieth century many of the classical traditions have been modified or replaced with

new ideas. Nevertheless, dozens of classical ballets choreographed in classical style continue to be seen on the stage.

Ballet is really a kind of theater. While the dancers are most important, stage settings, costumes, and choreography are all part of the art. The dance-dramas of ballet tell stories and express the thoughts and feelings of the characters in the ballet. Unlike music which cannot be lost once it is written down, many great dances are performed a few times and then are lost. A few systems of notating dance movements have been devised, but they are complicated and seldom used. Each choreographer has a unique way of planning a dance and communicating the steps to the performers. Most work from a general plan and then dem-

onstrate and discuss the dance patterns with the performers.

Music for ballet has interested composers of all eras. Usually composed for complete orchestra, the music often is performed in concert without dance. You may know the music and may have seen some of the most commonly produced ballets such as *The Nutcracker* with music composed by Tchaikovsky.

In class, talk about the ballets you have seen and the music you know. Ask a ballet student or teacher to demonstrate ballet positions and tell about dance choreography. Listen to the three contrasting musical compositions for ballet, read the following lessons, and engage in the dance activities suggested.

Dance of the Comedians

from *The Bartered Bride*

by Bedřich Smetana (1824-1884, Czechoslovakia)

Some of the best-known ballet music was written for operas. "Dance of the Comedians" is performed in a village festival scene. The "comedians" are dressed as circus performers. The village folk gather to watch the show. In the music the composer incorporated fiery Czech rhythms and melodies.

Listen to the music based on five themes. With letters, write the design in which the musical material is organized. What is the name of this familiar musical form? Suggest a circus act which might be dramatized in each section of the dance. Imagine the entire dance. Create your own dance-drama with the music.

Navarraise

from *Le Cid Ballet Suite*

by Jules Massenet (1842-1912, France)

The ballet music that Massenet composed for his opera *Le Cid* (The Chief) is often performed in orchestral concerts. Many characteristics of Spanish music are so well reproduced that the listener can easily imagine the scenes, dances, and instruments of Spain that inspired the French composer to write the music. The composer in his memoirs gave us this account: "I remember hearing in Spain the motif which begins the ballet. I was in the very country of Le Cid, living in a modest inn. It chanced that there was dancing all night in a lower room of the hotel. Several guitars and flutes repeated the dance tunes until they wore them out. I noted them down, a bit of color which I seized."

Inspired by the dances of the province of Navarre, this brilliant composition in $\frac{3}{4}$ meter is based on the unceasing sound of the rhythm.

$$\frac{3}{4} \quad \flat \quad \text{♪} \quad \text{♫} \quad \text{♫}$$

Above the rhythmic figure, the strings and other instruments play melodies which build in intensity and tempo and remind us of the most fiery Spanish dances we have seen. You can compose an interesting class dance with this music by using simple steps and swirls you have seen in Spanish dances. First, the boys might work out a stamping foot pattern with the rhythm of the music and plan line formations. A few girls might dance the short melody patterns of the first section and a larger group the swift, swirling patterns. When you have developed patterns you like, put them together in an original dance.

Infernal Dance of King Kastchei

from *The Firebird*

by Igor Stravinsky (1882-1971, Russia, USA)

Early in the twentieth century, Igor Stravinsky, one of the century's most prolific and well-known composers, began writing music that was a milestone in musical composition. Some of his finest compositions were for the ballet, and although they were sometimes too advanced to be accepted immediately, they are now among the most-performed ballets. *The Firebird* was first performed in Paris in 1910. It concerns a marvelous bird whose feathers are plumes of fire, and Prince Ivan, the hero of the ballet. Prince Ivan, wandering in an enchanted forest, sees the bird and tries to catch her, but succeeds only in plucking one flame from her coat. Coming upon the wild domain of the demon Kastchei, Ivan is surrounded by the demon's power and by other demons who would have killed him. The flame from the Firebird's coat protects him and the Firebird herself appears in the height of the battle to save him.

The music for Kastchei's dance in this scene is on your recording. Listen to it and imagine the dance scene. Later as you listen to the music several times, analyze the musical elements from which the description of the scene is derived: patterns of rhythm, melody, harmony, and instrumentation and dynamics. By following these musical elements and interpreting them, you might compose your own small group or class dance with the music.

179

In the twentieth century a new type of stage dance called "modern dance" has developed. In modern dance the movement often is expressed for its own sake and becomes the center of the art rather than a mere interpretation of stories. Some dancers have called it more "human." The movement is abstracted to express the desires and reactions of real people. The movement flows through time with little restriction from accompaniment.

Great simplicity marks modern dance. Costumes often are wraps, robes, or simple body covers. Often the stage is bare. The music usually is contemporary with sparse sound. Only a drum or a few instruments may be played as accompaniment to the dance. Expressive movement alone is the center of interest. Dancer and choreographer Martha Graham has been a leading exponent of modern dance since its beginning.

Doudlebska Polka

Folk Dance from Czechoslovakia

Music for the polka is popular in Czechoslovakia, and the polka circle dance is a typical dance of that country. Dances, such as the "Troika" of Russia and the French dance shown in the photographs above, are part of the folk-dance heritage that circles the world.

The "Doudlebska Polka" requires walking and polka steps. It is a "mixer" in which you will change partners with each completion of the three dance figures. Clapping, improvising on the movements, and loud singing along with the dance music are part of the Czech style.

Listen to the recording, and enjoy the folk-dance music in $\frac{2}{4}$ meter. Discover the ten sections of the music which follow a four-measure introduction. Each section is sixteen measures in length. Your teacher will give you directions for figures one, two, and three which you will dance with the first three sections of the music. With your record, the dance can be repeated.

Folk dance is the dance of the people. Styles of folk dances seem to be closely related to the place where people live and to their way of life. Even the clothing people wore had an influence. Full skirts inspired whirling and wooden shoes were good for stamping. The lederhosen (leather trousers) of Austrians were perfect for the thigh-slapping *schuhplattler* dances. The clacking dances on the cobbled streets of old mining towns required miners' clogs. From the heritage of climate, clothing, and general living patterns, each national or regional group developed dances that are unique. Folk dances are seen today on stage and screen as entertainment. People who belong to folk-dance clubs learn the dance patterns of different nations. In some areas, especially remote ones, folk dances are performed in village squares and rural settings much as they have been for hundreds of years.

Dances of India and other countries of the Far East are chiefly gesture dances and are related to religious rites. While dances of the West are full of drama and action, Eastern dances are quiet and contemplative. According to Hindu legend, the world was created in a divine dance, and since then the gods have continued to dance. The gesture language for dance was devised as early as the fifth century. The upper part of the body—the head, arms and fingers, and face—is most expressive. There are twenty-four movements for one hand, thirteen for two hands, ten arm movements, five chest movements, five movements for waist, thigh, and hip, some for neck and eyebrows, and thirty-six different glances that express different feelings. For example, if the thumb is bent and the fingers are outstretched, the hand position indicates clouds, river, waves, rainy season, sparkling water, or other ideas from the context of the drama. In India, Thailand, Cambodia, and other Asian countries the Temple Dances have preserved these ancient dance traditions. In Japan, the *No* and *Kubuki* dance-dramas were performed for royalty in the Imperial Palace for centuries. Since World War II, these have been seen in places of entertainment and are known to many travelers. Originally they were performed by men only. Masks or strange makeup and elaborate costumes are worn. Precise movements and basic positions result in finished performances.

Music and Your Career

Interest and skills in music developed early in your life can lead to an exciting business or professional career. Although comparatively few people have the unusual abilities and drive needed for a successful career as a composer, conductor, or professional performer, many use musical knowledge and skills in other interesting fields. You probably are aware of some of these; others, such as those discussed below, may be new to you.

Stage Manager

A stage manager works with a play or musical production, and during the performance, "runs the show." S/he reads the script and, if the production is an opera or musical, s/he must be familiar with the musical score as well. S/he knows how to use the technical equipment on the stage to meet the lighting and scenery requirements for each production. S/he works with the set designer, the stage crew, and, to some extent, with performers. In most cases, a stage manager has studied dramatics and theater arts. If s/he wishes to work in musical productions, s/he must study the stage works of numerous composers, watch many performances, and get as much experience as possible in school productions.

S/he must be able to plan and organize complicated changes of scenery quickly and efficiently. S/he must often work under the pressures of very precise timing, working with many people. The schedule of a stage manager may be very demanding. In a busy theater or opera house, s/he may have to see that the stage sets for a previous show are removed in the morning, then set up the stage and run the lights for an afternoon rehearsal of a second show, and finally, run the evening performance of yet another production. People who do such work in the theater often say they have "theater in their blood." They are stimulated by the opportunity to help create a beautiful performance for an audience.

Artist and Concert Manager

A manager runs a kind of employment agency; s/he develops contacts and schedules appearances for performers and performing groups. There usually are available many more performers than concert dates, and the manager tries to get as many good contracts as possible for each of the artists. S/he must know each musician's repertoire, the kind of audience s/he suits best, the amount of travel s/he desires, the number of engagements s/he needs. S/he must have broad contacts in the music world in order to hear of new artists. The manager must know the music scene across the country, where tickets to concerts can be sold, and the types of concert each community likes. S/he prepares the day-to-day schedule and itinerary for the artists and makes arrangements for them. S/he furnishes photographs, brochures, and information to local people who will sell tickets for the concert.

The concert manager often has an agency with several employees: a person in charge of promotion, a person to prepare the printed programs, a travel manager, and a bookkeeper. A manager should have a background in music, be able to work 'with figures and dates, and have administrative ability. Some managers work with one musical group only. They travel with the musicians and manage the many details of schedule, travel, programs, and records.

Choreographer

A choreographer combines elements of movement, space, and music into dance. S/he must have an extensive knowledge of dance; in fact most choreographers have been or are dancers. S/he must know music and be familiar with music literature, as s/he may be required to choose the music for the dance or show. Often s/he has studied theater arts as well.

Choreography is required in all forms of dance: ballet, modern, tap, and acrobatic dance. It is needed in opera, concerts, musical comedy, television and films, in professional and community theater, and in night club acts. Directors of shows for industrial promotion and television advertising also frequently hire choreographers.

A choreographer has a knowledge of people—knowledge of the dancer or actor and how s/he can best achieve an idea in movement, and knowledge of people in the audience and how they will react to what the dancer does. The choreographer may study in a professional dance school, in a university, or both. In preparation for this profession, s/he will observe shows of many different types and learn from other choreographers.

Which other businesses and professions related to music do you know about? In a class discussion, exchange information about those listed below. Invite members of some of the professions to come to your class. Prepare a plan and use a tape recorder to interview some interesting people. Share your interviews in class.

- Music Therapist
- Music Librarian in a college or public library, for a radio or TV station, for an orchestra or band
- Owner or employee of a music store
- Record Producer
- Music Journalist
- Music Teacher in a public or private school, private studio, college or university
- Program Director or Disc Jockey for a radio station

more songs to sing

Aquarius/Let the Sun Shine In

Music by Galt MacDermot
Words by James Rado and
Gerome Ragni

When the moon _____ is in the sev-enth house, _____ and
Ju-pi-ter _____ a-ligns with Mars, _____ Then peace _____
_____ will guide the _ plan-ets, _____ And love _____ will steer the stars; _
_____ This is the dawn-ing of the age of A-qua-ri-us,
age of A-qua-ri-us, _____ A-qua-ri-us, _____
_____ A-qua-ri-us! _____

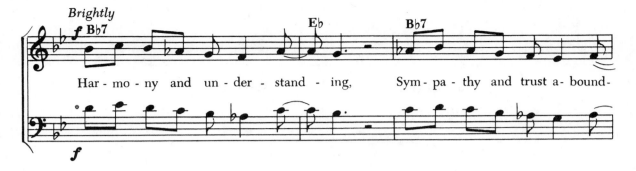

Har - mo - ny and un - der - stand - ing, Sym - pa - thy and trust a - bound -

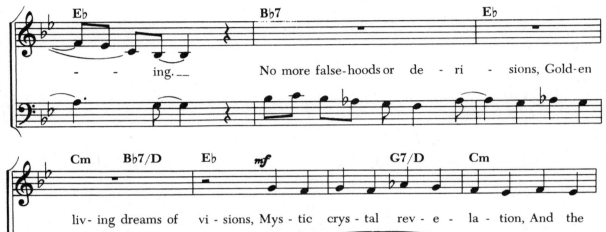

- ing. ___ No more false-hoods or de - ri - sions, Gold - en

liv - ing dreams of vi - sions, Mys - tic crys - tal rev - e - la - tion, And the

oo ___

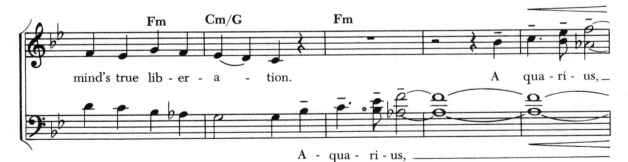

mind's true lib - er - a - tion. A qua - ri - us, ___

A - qua - ri - us,

A - qua - ri - us! ___ When the

smoothly

190

Coda
F
Cm
A - qua - ri - us,
A - qua - ri - us!
Soulfully
1.
2.
3
4.
Let the sun shine, Let the sun shine in, the sun shine in.
Let the sun shine, Let the sun shine in, the sun shine in.
Melody
TRUMPET OR CLARINET
Clap
RHYTHM
TAMBOURINE
Gm
D7
Eb
Bb
Repeat ad lib. until fade-out.

Here are some patterns to play at the beginning of "Aquarius," while the Cm7 chord is being held. The recording of these songs by the "Fifth Dimension" has been extremely popular.

The Fifth Dimension

Up and Get Us Gone

Music by William J. Reynolds
Words by Ed Seabough
Arr. B. A. R.

This song could be called a modern American folk song. Play these patterns as an accompaniment.

1. Up, my neigh-bor, come a-way, See the world that's ours to-day, ___ The war-ring place, ___ the starv-ing child, ___ The lone-ly ones, ___ the group gone ___ wild! ___

2. Up, my neigh-bor, see the worth, Heed the call and speak the truth, ___ To seek to know, ___ to find a way, ___ To help a man ___ this ver-y ___ day.

Up, my neigh-bor, see the land, See the ghet-to how it stands, ___ The crowd-ed room, ___ the lit-tered filth, ___ The

Up, my neigh-bor, leave this place, Peo-ple now of ev-ery race ___ Have need of love ___ that you can give, ___ Have

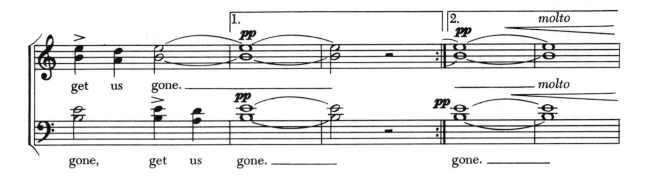

get us gone. _____

gone, get us gone. _____ gone. _____

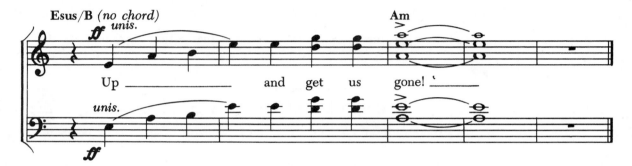

Up _____ and get us gone! _____

Donovan Leitch

Jenifer Juniper

Words and Music
by Donovan Leitch
Arr. B. A. R.

ver - y low.
ev - er so.

(melody in lower voice)

What-cha do - in', Jen - i - fer, my love?
What-cha do - in', Jen - i - fer, my love?

3. I'm think-ing of what it would be like if

she loved me. You know, just late - ly, this hap - py song,

It came a - long, and I like to some - how try and tell you:

4. Jen - i - fer Jun - i - per, Hair of gold - en flax,
5. Jen - i - fer Jun - i - per, vit sur la col - line,

Jen - i - fer Jun - i - per Longs for what she lacks.
Jen - i - fer Jun - i - per, as - si - se très tran - quille.

Listen to Donovan's performances of his three songs and of "Get Thy Bearings" on page 19. Make observations about the songs, the singing style, and the instrumental accompaniment. Which song reminds you of an English folk song? In which song does the singing style imitate an instrument? In which accompaniments are orchestral instruments featured? What do they contribute to the accompaniment? Why do you think the rock style, jazz, and the more simple accompaniments were selected for each particular song?

Hurdy Gurdy Man

Words and Music
by Donovan Leitch
Arr. B. A. R.

Steadily droning on

Oh _____

1. Thrown like a star in my __ vast sleep I
2. His - to- ries __ of ag - es past __

o - pen   my eyes ___ to take ___ a   peep ___
un - en - - light - ened ___ shad - ows cast ___

To find ___ that I ___ was by ___ the sea, ___
Down __ through all ___ e - ter - ni - ty, ___ the

gaz - ing   with tran - quil - i - ty. ___ 'Twas
cry - ing   of hu - man - i - ty. ___ 'Tis

then   when the Hur - dy Gur - dy Man __ came
then   when the Hur - dy Gur - dy Man __ comes

sing - ing songs of   love, ___ Then when the Hur - dy Gur - dy Man __ came
sing - ing songs of   love, ___ Then when the Hur - dy Gur - dy Man __ comes

198

sing - ing   songs _____   of   love. _____
sing - ing   songs _____   of   love. _____

Hur - dy gur - dy hur - dy gur - dy hur - dy gur - dy, gur - dy he sang, _____

Hur - dy gur - dy hur - dy gur - dy hur - dy gur - dy, gur - dy he sang, _____

Hur - dy gur - dy hur - dy gur - dy hur - dy gur - dy, gur - dy he sang, _____

Hur - dy gur - dy hur - dy gur - dy hur - dy gur - dy, gur - dy he sang, _____

Here comes the ro - ly po - ly man_ and he's sing - ing songs of love, _____

Ro - ly po - ly ro - ly po - ly, po - ly ro - ly po - ly he sang. _____

The Entertaining of a Shy Little Girl

Words and Music
by Donovan Leitch
Arr. B. A. R.

Add the following bell part as an accompaniment for this song.

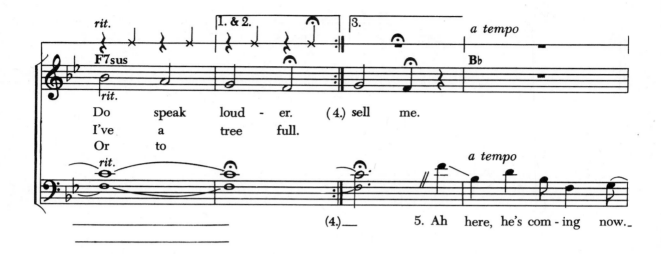

Do speak loud - er. (4.) sell me.
I've a tree full.
Or to

(4.)___ 5. Ah here, he's com - ing now.

Squeak, ___ Squeak. ___ Tah, ___ Tah. ___

I'll say cheer - i - o!

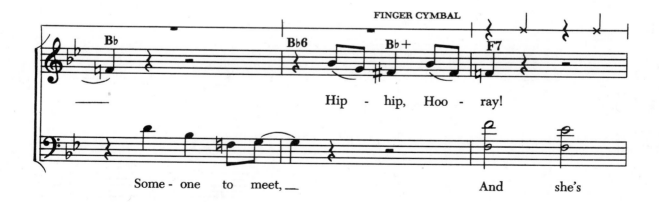

Hip - hip, Hoo - ray!

Some - one to meet, ___ And she's

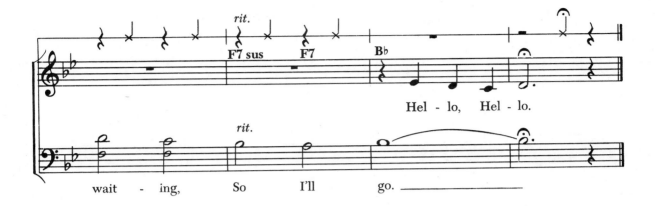

Green Fields

Words and Music
by Terry Gilkyson, Rick Dehr,
and Frank Miller
Arr. by Fred Bock

Slowly, with a steady beat

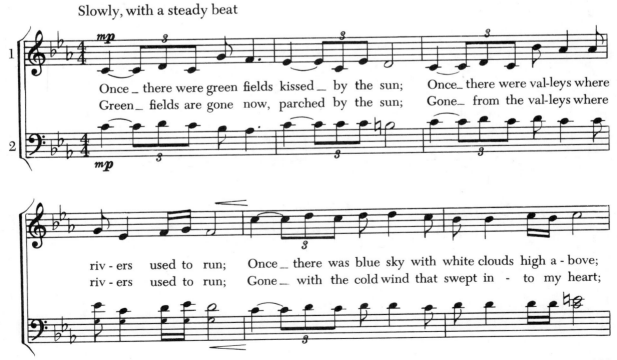

Once ___ they were part of an ev-er-last - ing love.
Gone ___ with the lov-ers who let their dreams ___ de-part.

We ___ were the lov-ers who strolled through green fields. ___
Where ___ are the green fields that we used to roam? ___

I'll ___ nev-er know what made you run a-way. How can I keep search-ing when

dark clouds hide the day? I on - ly know there's noth-ing here for me,

Noth-ing in this wide world left for me to see. But I'll ___ keep on wait-ing

'til __ you re - turn, I'll __ keep on wait - ing un - til the day you learn

You can't be hap-py while your heart's on the roam. You can't be hap-py un -

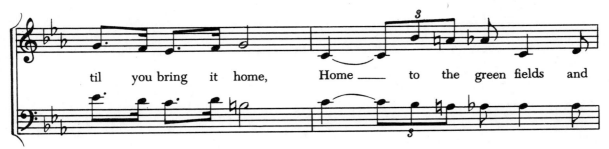

til you bring it home, Home __ to the green fields and

me once a - gain. ____ Home to the green fields a - gain.

All Lands and Peoples

Music by Austin C. Lovelace
Words by Stophord A. Brooke
(Based on Psalm 100)

All lands and peoples of the earth,
Put off your night of sadness;
Make cheer, and music, and high mirth;
And praise the Lord with gladness!

Serve him with joyful heart,
All kingdoms do their parts,
And let immortal song
Before his presence throng,
Forever and forever.

Summer Song

Words and Music
by Dave Brubeck

With lazy motion

Noth - ing else ___ is like a sum-mer day; When ___ it's gone, ___ the
I'm ___ for sum - mer! That's my time of year; Win - ter shad - ows

mem - o - ries will stay. Life ___ so free ___ and eas - y! ___ Friend-ly
fade and dis - ap - pear. When ___ it's warm ___ and peace-ful, ___ When the

1.
clouds are float - ing high in a la - zy sum - mer sky.

2.
rit. *after D.S. to Coda* *a tempo*
days are grow - ing long, I can sing my sum - mer song. ___

fish - in' ___
I hear laugh - ter from the swim-min' hole: ___ Kids out fish - in'

with a wil - low pole: Boats come drift - in' round the bend.

poco rit. D.S. *Coda* *pp*
a tempo
Why must sum - mer ___ ev - er end? ___ song, my sum - mer song.

Surfing Song

Music by Princess Likelike
English Words by B. L.

Slowly

On the o - cean, with the waves for - ev - er roll - ing, I hear the
Ku-'u i - po i - ka he-'e pu-'e - o - ne, Me-ke ka.- i ne-he

tale of long a - go: ____ Of the surf - er, a great and might-y
i - ka 'i-li-'i-li, Ni-po a - ku i-la-i-la ka ma-

chief - tain, Of the prin-cess, and love she would be - stow.____
na - 'o, U-a ki-li-'o-pu ma-ua i ka na-he - le.

REFRAIN

Rise, waves, and lift me ev - er sky - ward, I am glid - ing,
Ei a - la e ma-li-u ma - i, E____ i-a ke a-

glid - ing toward the shore.____ Rise, waves, and lift me with your
lo - ha i - a'e ne - i. Hi - ki mai a - na i - ka po

pow - er, I am glid-ing, Let me glide for - ev - er-more.____
ne - i, U-a ki-li-'o-pu ma-u-a i ka na he - le.

O God, Our Help in Ages Past

Music Attributed to William Croft
Words by Isaac Watts
Arr. B. A. R.

Climactic—strict tempo

our de - fence is sure. Be - fore the hills in

our de - fence is sure.

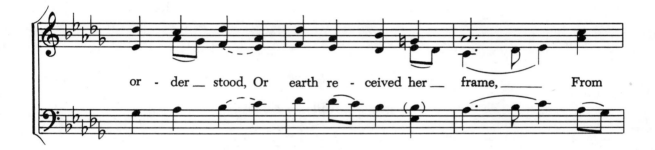

or - der stood, Or earth re - ceived her frame, From

rit. *ten.*

ev - er - last - ing thou art God, To end-less years the same.

rit. *ten.*

Allegro—spirited

O God, our help in ag - es past, Our

For Us a Child Is Born

Anonymous Round

For us a Child is born this day, No - ël,_____

_____ No - ël, No - ël, No - ël, No - ël!

A Christmas Happening

by Buryl A. Red

Deck the hall with boughs of holly, Fa la la la la, la
Fa _____ la la la

la la la, _____ 'Tis the sea - son to _____ be jol - ly,
la la la,

Fa la la la la, la la la la. ____
Fa _____ la la la la la la. ____

Sing we joy - ous all _____ to - geth - er, Fa la la, la la la,
Sing we all _____ to - geth - er, Fa la la, la

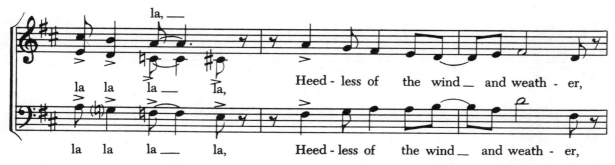

la, _____
la la la _____ la, Heed - less of the wind _____ and weath - er,
la la la _____ la, Heed - less of the wind _____ and weath - er,

An - gels we have heard on high,___ Sweet-ly___ sing - ing___

o'er the plains, And the moun - tains___ in re - ply___

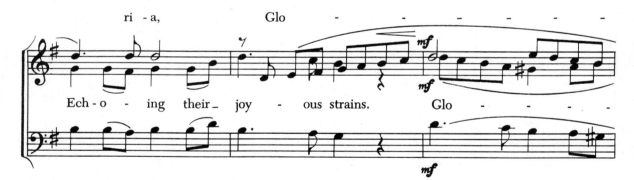

Ech - o - ing their___ joy - ous strains. Glo - - -

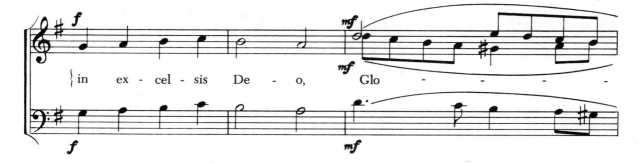

in ex - cel - sis De - o, Glo

ri - a

in ex - cel - sis De - o.

Ah._____

Peace on earth!__   Peace on earth!_

(*French*)
Paix sur la terre!
(*Pè sir la tèrr*)

(*Spanish*)
Paz en la tierra!
(*Pass en la tyérra*)

Repeat ad lib

__ Peace on earth!_   Peace on earth!_   Peace on earth!_

(*Swahili*)
Amani iwe duniani!
(*Ahmahnee eé-way doonyahnee*)

(*Italian*)
Pace in terra!
(*Pahchay een tehrrah*)

(*German*)
Friede auf Erden!
(*Freéduh owf Airdun*)

(*Russian*)
Mir na zemle!
(*Mihr nah zehmleh*)

Repeat ad lib

Music by Buryl Red ★ Book and Lyrics by Grace Hawthorne

A musical for S.A.B. or S.A. chorus

REVOLUTIONARY IDEAS

PART I

PART I

SETTING: *The living room of a typical New England home. A large fireplace equipped with cooking pots, andirons, a wooden bucket filled with logs, dominates the warm, comfortable room. The time is December, 1773.*

A group of teenagers is seated casually around the room talking.

"Revolutionary Ideas"

Grace Hawthorne

Buryl Red

219

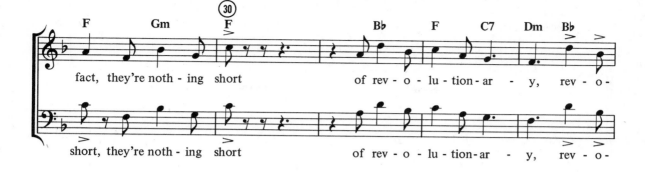

fact, they're noth - ing short of rev - o - lu - tion - ar - y, rev - o -

short, they're noth - ing short of rev - o - lu - tion - ar - y, rev - o -

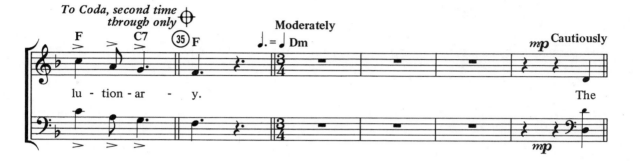

To Coda, second time through only

Moderately

lu - tion - ar - y. The

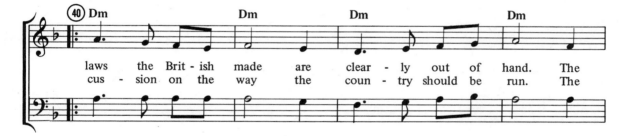

laws the Brit - ish made are clear - ly out of hand. The
cus - sion on the way the coun - try should be run. The

With growing assertiveness

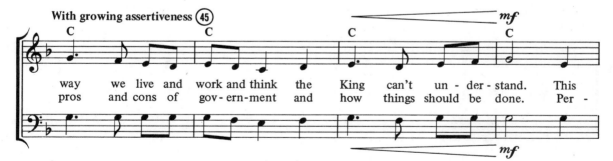

way we live and work and think the King can't un - der - stand. This
pros and cons of gov - ern - ment and how things should be done. Per -

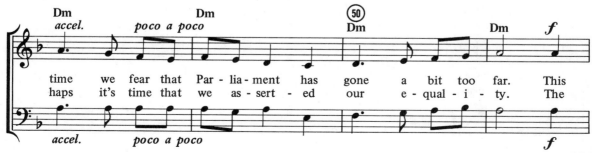

time we fear that Par - lia - ment has gone a bit too far. This
haps it's time that we as - sert - ed our e - qual - i - ty. The

accel. *poco a poco*

221

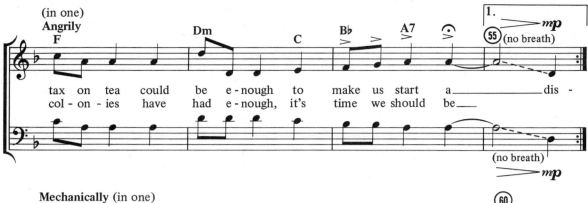

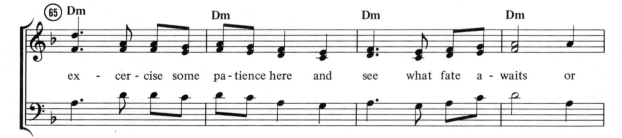

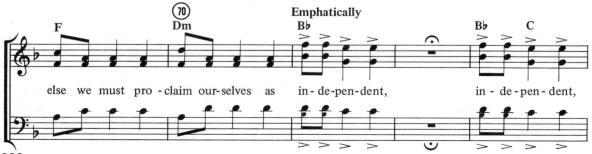

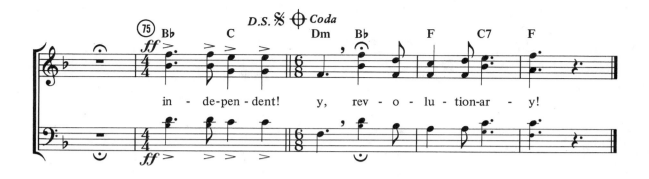

GEORGE:	You better be careful of what you say.
JOHN:	What? I'm not saying anything. But we are different. I mean, I have a cousin in London, same age as me and everything. He came here last summer, and we couldn't even understand each other.
MARK:	Oh well sure, I can't understand my cousins either, and they just live in Georgia.
JOHN:	I don't mean the way they talk; I mean we didn't think the same. We could both do the same thing, and it was still . . . *(at a loss for words)* . . . different.
MARTHA:	Oh, come on, John, you're British just like everyone else, and I . . .
RUTH:	My dad talks just like John. Sure, we're British—but we're different too.
MARTHA:	My family never talked much until lately. Now they talk all the time—about being "different," whatever that means. And taxes and embargoes. They say what applies to England doesn't apply to us.
BETSY:	Even my dad says we were better off when they left us alone.
RUTH:	My family was really mad about all those import taxes.
BETSY:	But we took care of that. We stopped importing anything that had a duty on it.
JOHN:	Yeah, and it worked too. They repealed the duties.
GEORGE:	Not quite. There's still the tea.
RUTH:	No matter. My mother says we just won't drink tea. I can't believe how involved she is in all this.
BETSY:	My mother and a lot of her friends signed this petition saying they weren't going to buy tea or wear English-made clothing . . . boy, did my father have a fit, but Mom didn't care. She's really serious about this.
JOHN:	*(knowingly)* There are better things to do than just sign petitions.
RUTH:	What does that mean?
JOHN:	Oh, nothing.
RUTH:	*(Motions to girls to join her in another part of the room, speaks mockingly.)* Well there are better things to talk about than nothing. Come on, I've got something . . .
JOHN:	*(waits till they are out of hearing distance and then speaks cautiously)* Do any of you know about a . . . tea party? *(Several boys nod their heads "yes.")*
MARK:	Are you going?
JOHN:	You bet I am! Do you realize this will be the first time we've stood up to the British, the first time we've done anything?
GEORGE:	What are you talking about?
JOHN:	You know those three ships that are full of tea, the ones that have been sitting in Boston Harbor for two weeks; well, tonight we're going to unload them.

GEORGE: Unload them?—but I thought the point was to keep them <u>from</u> being unloaded.

JOHN: . . . unload them right into Boston Harbor. My father and men from all around are going to dress like Indians and <u>raid those ships</u>.

GEORGE: But won't there be trouble?

JOHN: No! Absolutely not. It's all very well planned, just open the boxes, pour into the bay . . . and instant tea. *(The girls come back to join the conversation.)* The biggest tea party in the world.

RUTH: What did you say about a tea party?

MARK: John is . . . *(looks around, then adds boastfully)* . . . I mean, we're <u>all</u> going to a tea.

"When Invited to a Tea"

Grace Hawthorne

Buryl Red

Solo or group; male or female (preferably male, sounding an octave lower).

gen-tle and po-lite and calm, one must not un-seem-ly be._____ And these

so-cial gra-ces must__ a-bound, when in-vit-ed to__ a__

tea, (hee, hee) when in-vit-ed to__ a__ tea (hee, hee, hee, hee, hee, hee, hee).

(hee, hee, hee,   hee,   hee).

third time to Coda in tempo

Stately **Elegantly** (minuet)

1. First ar - rive   on   time   at   the   right   ad -
2. If   you   must   dis - cuss   keep   your   chat - ter

dress, (It's the   Old South Meet-ing   Hall...) And con - duct your-self   with__
light, (We won't   need to   talk   at   all...) Sit with   spe - cial   care, keep your

gra - cious - ness; (We'll as - sem - ble at night - fall...) And be   care - ful
head   up - right; (We will   all   be stand - ing tall...) When the   tea   is

*If sung by treble voices only, altos should sing part in brackets ⌐ ¬.
 If sung by mixed voices, all treble voices should sing part in brackets ⌐ ¬.

**If sung by treble voices only, altos sing middle line, sopranos sing top line in brackets ⌐ ¬.
  If sung by mixed voices, omit top line and all treble voices sing middle line in brackets ⌐ ¬.

Blackout. All characters with speaking parts exit.

227

This scene takes place two years after the Boston Tea Party.
The time is spring, 1775.

JOHN, GEORGE, and BETSY and MARK enter.

JOHN: *(as if finishing a sentence)* . . . I still think about it. There must have been 70 or 80 of us and hundreds of thousands watching . . . well, thousands anyway.

GEORGE: And we only damaged one padlock.

MARK: Boy, 342 chests of tea. I never worked so hard in my life.

JOHN: That tea was worth £18,000. What a night. I'm going to tell my grandchildren about that.

BETSY: If you live that long.

MARK: What does that mean?

BETSY: It means that the tea party was just that—a party—fun, not like what's happening now. After Lexington and Concord, it can't be fun anymore . . . *(softly)* . . . it's war.

There's a moment's pause, and then the other girls enter and take places around the room.

JOHN: *(trying to ignore the interruption)* But we couldn't do anything else. Now the Continental Congress has gotten off its . . . chairs and started doing something too.

BETSY: I wish I lived in Philadelphia, so I could meet all those men in Congress — Hancock and Adams and Jefferson and Lee. I wish I didn't just have to <u>read</u> about it.

MARK: Oh, come on, this is serious.

BETSY: *(surprised)* I <u>am</u> serious. I'm the only one around here who <u>is</u> serious.

GEORGE: Not quite. Anyway, John is right. Now Congress is doing something. They're going to take responsibility for the army, and they've appointed that man from Virginia—Washington—to command it.

BETSY: I wish I lived in Virginia.

MARK: Oh good grief!

BETSY: No, you <u>think</u> about it. All we do is talk, but it was a Virginian who was the first president of the Continental Congress, and it's a Virginian who's going to command the Army, and I'll bet, if anybody ever has enough nerve to ask Congress to vote for independence—that will be a Virginian too.

GEORGE: How about John Adams?

BETSY: Oh Adams, Smadams. Everyone knows he's 100% for independence, but he talks so <u>much</u>, I don't think anyone listens. But when that other guy from Virginia . . . ah . . . Patrick Henry—when he talks, <u>every</u> <u>word</u> counts. When he said "Give me liberty, or give me death," <u>everybody</u> listened.

GEORGE: Well, I hope you're right. I hope everybody <u>did</u> listen, because I think that's the only choice we have left. We've come too far to stop now.

*During the musical introduction, characters form a tableau
which is maintained throughout the song.*

"The Sea of Liberty"

Grace Hawthorne

Buryl Red

GIRLS

1. The_____ spring_of_____ free - dom
   stream_of_____ free - dom

BOYS

(for second verse only) 2. Free - dom

bub - bles_forth in qui - et ser - en - i - ty. And_____
flows_a - long, it cuts through_rock and clay. It_____

flows a - long through rock and_ clay.

at its source it's fresh and clear and pure._____ So_____
nev - er stops no mat - ter what the cost._____ It_____

No mat - ter what the cost.

Oh_____ Oh_____

like a spring it must move on its jour - ney to the_____
gath - ers strength from rains of truth that fall from day to_____

Oh_____ that falls from_____

Preferably, first verse should be sung by male voices only, reading from treble clef, sounding an octave lower than written.
**If first verse is sung by mixed chorus, treble voices should sing top notes; bass voices, bottom notes.*
 If sung by treble chorus only, treble voices divide.

*Treble voices only.
**If sung by treble chorus only, lower voices sing bottom staff, upper voices divide on top staff.
If sung by mixed chorus, bass voices sing lower staff, sounding an octave lower than written.
***Cue notes indicate optional part for male voices only; to be sounded an octave lower than written.

230

*If sung by treble chorus only, voices divide, lower part sings cue notes.
If sung by mixed chorus, treble voices divide, lower part sings cue notes; bass voices sing top line an octave lower than written; cue notes represent optional bass part to be sung an octave lower than written.

rit. ⑤⓪

count the cost of find - ing truth, con - sid - er if you___

mp cresc.
The

a tempo With vigor *

dare. The___ spring of free-dom must

The___ spring of free-dom must flow,_____ must

⑤⑤

spring of free - dom must flow,_____ must

flow,_____ must flow,_____ must

flow, free - dom must flow,_____ must

rit. _____ f Broadly

flow,_____ must flow__ to the sea__ of__ lib - er - ty.

rit. _____ f

*If sung by treble chorus only, voices should
sing these bars in place of above:

cresc.
mp The___ spring of free-dom must

The___ spring of free-dom must___ flow,_____ must

Blackout.

Everyone but JOHN is on stage at the beginning of the next scene. A new character, WAYNE, is seated next to MARTHA.

JOHN: *(bursts into the room)* I've done it! I'm in! I've joined the Army!

ALL: *(Everyone crowds around JOHN, and all speak at once.)* When? For how long? When do you leave? Where will you go? Where's your uniform?

JOHN: Hey, wait a minute. I don't know where I'm going; I don't even know much about the army.

MARTHA: Well, tell us what you do know.

MARK: *(skeptically)* When do you get a uniform?

BETSY: If he's like most people, he won't get one. He'll wear just what he has on and bring his own musket.

JOHN: *(reluctantly)* Yeah, that's right, but I'm getting paid $7.33 a month. Actually, just a few of the regiments have uniforms. What everybody does is to wear a sprig of laurel in their hats, and at night they replace it with a piece of white paper. *(unceratin pause)* Well, that's what I heard.

MARTHA: What else have you heard?

JOHN: I not only heard this, I got it! *(pulls a $20 bill out of his pocket)* Twenty dollars! That's a bonus just for enlisting, and if I serve during the war, I get 100 acres of land when it's over.

MARK: Where?

JOHN: Where, what?

MARK: You get 100 acres of land—where?

JOHN: *(realizes that he hasn't considered this)* Well . . . I don't know.

BETSY: *(knowingly)* I thought privates just made $6.00.

JOHN: I make more, 'cause I enlisted as a drummer. And if I get to be a drum major, I'll make $8.00 a month. That's as much as a regular sergeant.

MARK: Maybe they'll give you one of those new Pennsylvania rifles. Those things shoot so far you wouldn't even have to leave home.

JOHN: No, Betsy is right; I have to bring my own gun, *(eagerly)* but I get $2 more if I bring a blanket.

MARK: Boy, I wish I could go.

BETSY: I wish you could too.

JOHN: As far as I'm concerned, you can all go, but if you're going, you better get ready. Come on, we'll form a company band. *(JOHN grabs the bucket from the fireplace and tucks it under his arm and beats the bottom like a bass drum.)* Segue to music.

"Join Up"

Grace Hawthorne

Buryl Red

234

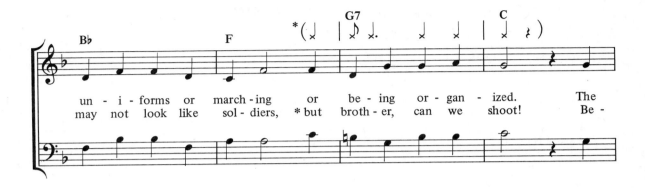

(♩ | ♪ ♩. ♩ ♩ | ♩ 𝄽)

G7　　　　　　　**C**

B♭　　　　　　　**F**

un - i - forms or march - ing　or　be - ing or - gan - ized.　The
may not look like sol - diers, *but broth - er, can we shoot!　Be -

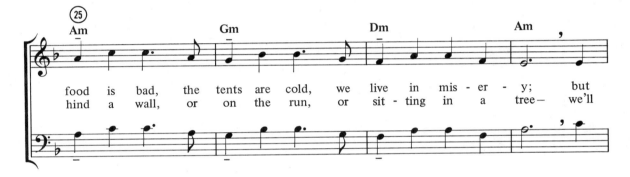

㉕ **Am**　　　　**Gm**　　　　**Dm**　　　　**Am**

food is bad, the tents are cold, we live in mis - er - y;　but
hind a wall, or on the run, or sit - ting in a tree — we'll

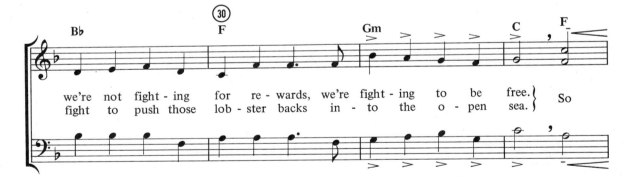

B♭　　　　㉚ **F**　　　　**Gm**　　　　**C**　　**F**

we're not fight - ing for re - wards, we're fight - ing to be free.} So
fight to push those lob - ster backs in - to the o - pen sea.}

f **B♭**　　　　**F**　　　　�35 **Gm**　　　　**F**

join up　and bring your ken, we want you in the Min - ute Men.

f

This phrase should be shouted in second verse.

235

Join up and bring your ken, we want you in the Min - ute Men.

March Routine

CYMBALS and SNARE DRUM
BASS DRUM

JOHN

"Come on, get up! You're going to learn to march!"

1. The Bri - tish know how to
(2.) gen - 'rals are al - ways

CHORUS

dress.
fat.

They're no - ted for march - ing too.
The priv - ates are al - ways lean.

We'll
The

You're right!

You're right!

have to go and win the war, it's all that we can do!
gen - 'rals eat the fan - cy stuff, and we eat all the beans.

Hey,

Repeat these bars as needed to prepare for march.
**No specific pitch.*

236

count off!   Count   off!   One, two,   three, four,

One,   two!   Three, four! One, two,   three, four,

**To Coda second
time through**

(disgustedly)

One,   two,   three, four.   Let's go back and

SOLO **   CHORUS (questioningly)

Five,   six!   Five, six?

count some more.   2. The

Four, three, two, one, that's the way it should be done.

* In a chanting fashion throughout; pitches indicate inflection only.
**One voice rather stubbornly.

*Same voice, this time with pride.

239

want you in the Min-ute Men. Join up and bring your ken; we

want you in the Min - ute Men._____ JOHN: We're ____

off to win the war To make this chor-us rhyme We'll

You're right! You're right!

have to whip the Brit - ish and be home by sup - per time. So

*No specific pitch.

240

JOHN:	Anybody else want to come? *(For the first time, he notices WAYNE sitting with Martha.)*
MARTHA:	Ah . . . this is my cousin, Wayne.
JOHN:	*(taunting)* Well, Wayne, want to join up?
WAYNE:	I already have. I'm just home on furlough. *(All attention turns to Wayne.)*
JOHN:	*(dejectedly)* Oh.
OTHERS:	Where were you? What did you do? Did you fight?
WAYNE:	I didn't exactly fight; I'm a courier. I take messages from the field to the Congress.
BETSY:	*(very impressed)* Congress! You mean you've been there? You know everyone?
WAYNE:	I've seen most of them. . . .
RUTH:	Tell us what they're like.
MARTHA:	Oh well, Wayne may not want to. . . .
GEORGE:	But we really want to know what they're like.
WAYNE:	Well, I'll try. Let's see, there are the Adams cousins.
GEORGE:	Samuel and John.
WAYNE:	Yes. They both talk a lot. In fact, John Adams has been talking about independence almost every time I've seen him.
BETSY:	See, I told you so.
WAYNE:	*(patiently)* And there's John Hancock. He's rich. You can tell by the way he dresses. He's the President of the Congress, you know.
JOHN:	*(trying not to be impressed)* We know.
WAYNE:	Then, there's Dickinson—John, I think his name is. Anyway, he's always arguing with Adams. I don't think Dickinson wants independence.
GEORGE:	Why not?
WAYNE:	I don't know. Oh, and there's the old man, Mr. Franklin. He's funny. No matter what's going on, he'll make some wise remark. Somebody told me they wouldn't let him write the declaration because they were afraid he would put a joke in it.
RUTH:	So, who's writing it?
WAYNE:	It's already written. Thomas Jefferson did it, and now they're trying to vote on it.
BETSY:	I'll bet he's from Virginia, isn't he? *(She hardly waits for an answer.)*
WAYNE:	Yes.
BETSY:	I knew it. I told you that too.
GEORGE:	*(to Betsy)* Yeah, but it will be Adams who pushes to get it passed.
JOHN:	What happens when they vote on it?
WAYNE:	If they vote yes, we'll have declared ourselves . . . free and independent states.
MARK:	*(disappointed)* Then that will be the end of it.
GEORGE:	Oh no, declaring freedom and winning freedom are two different things. This will just be the beginning.

"Independence Now, Independence Forever"

Spoken Excerpts: Patrick Henry and Daniel Webster
Lyrics: Grace Hawthorne

Music: Buryl Red

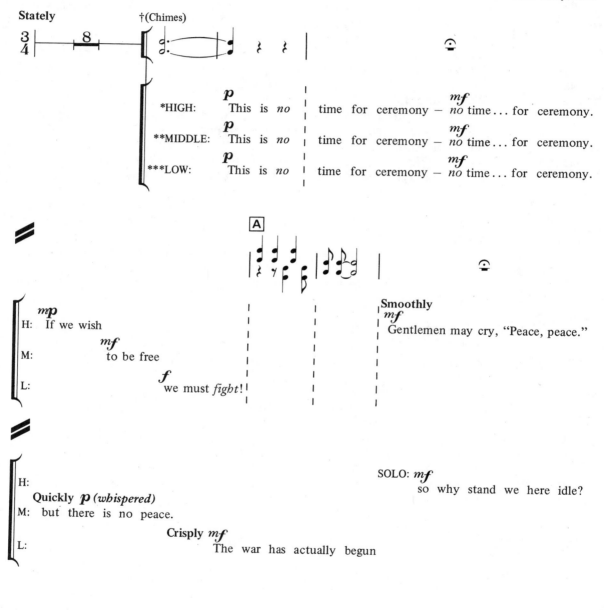

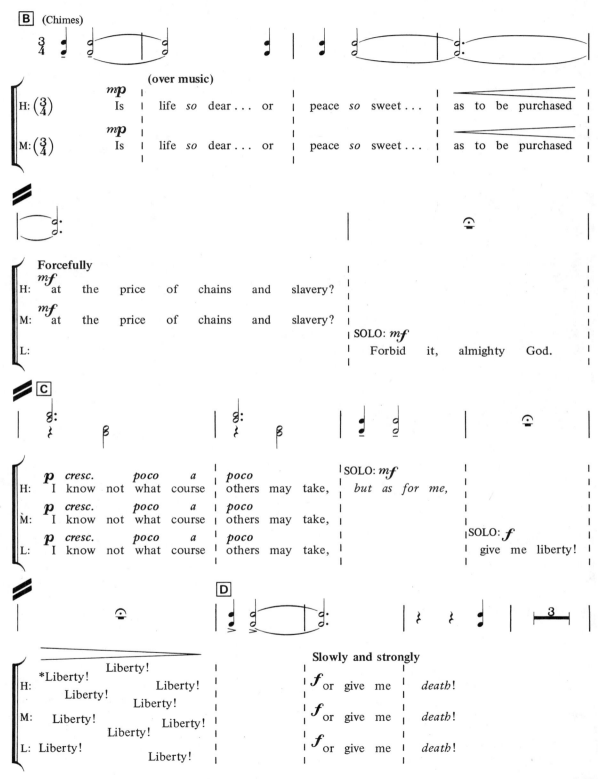

B (Chimes)

(over music)

mp
H: (3/4)   Is | life *so* dear ... or | peace *so* sweet ... | as to be purchased |

mp
M: (3/4)   Is | life *so* dear ... or | peace *so* sweet ... | as to be purchased |

Forcefully
mf
H: at the price of chains and slavery? |

mf
M: at the price of chains and slavery? |

L: | SOLO: *mf* Forbid it, almighty God. |

C

p cresc. *poco* *a* | *poco* | SOLO: *mf*
H: I know not what course | others may take, | *but as for me,*

p cresc. *poco* *a* | *poco*
M: I know not what course | others may take, |

p cresc. *poco* *a* | *poco* | SOLO: *f*
L: I know not what course | others may take, | give me liberty! |

D

Slowly and strongly

*Liberty!
Liberty!   Liberty!
H: *Liberty! | *f* or give me | *death!*
      Liberty!
      Liberty!
M: Liberty!   Liberty! | *f* or give me | *death!*
            Liberty!
L: Liberty! | *f* or give me | *death!*
                  Liberty!

*Individual voices repeat ad lib in rapid succession to give an echoing effect.

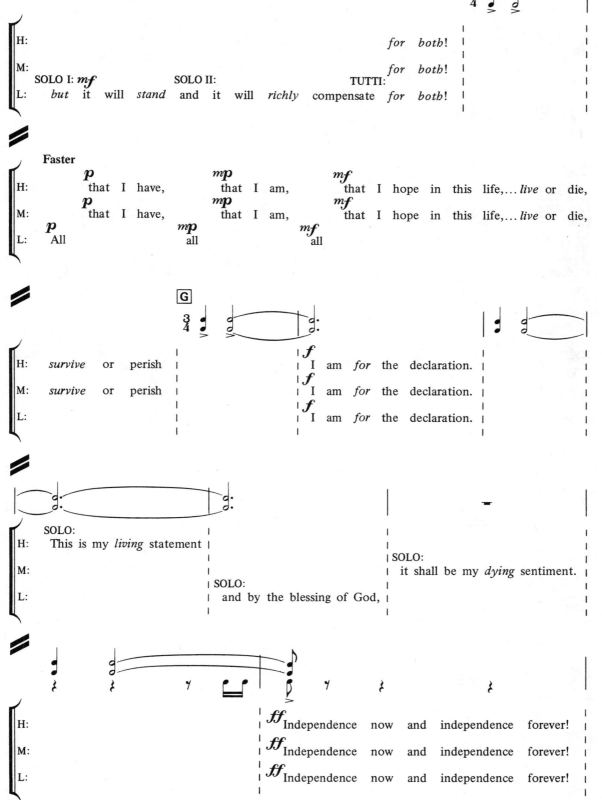

H: for both!

M: for both!

SOLO I: *mf* SOLO II: TUTTI:
L: *but* it will *stand* and it will *richly* compensate *for both*!

Faster

p *mp* *mf*
H: that I have, that I am, that I hope in this life,... *live* or die,
p *mp* *mf*
M: that I have, that I am, that I hope in this life,... *live* or die,
p *mp* *mf*
L: All all all

G

H: *survive* or perish *f* I am *for* the declaration.
M: *survive* or perish *f* I am *for* the declaration.
L: *f* I am *for* the declaration.

SOLO:
H: This is my *living* statement
SOLO:
M: it shall be my *dying* sentiment.
SOLO:
L: and by the blessing of God,

ff
H: Independence now and independence forever!
ff
M: Independence now and independence forever!
ff
L: Independence now and independence forever!

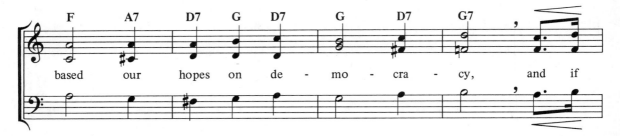

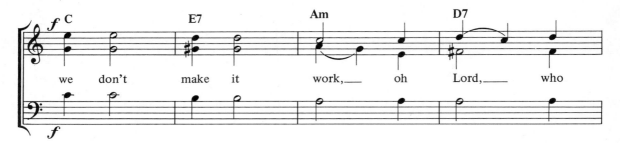

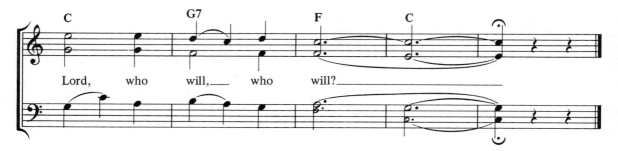

*To end musical here, sing "If We Don't Make It Work, Who Will?" from Exploring Music, Book 8.   **end of part 1**

THE END PART 1

Supplementary Glossary

Antiphony Music in which two groups of singers and/or instrumentalists alternate responsively.

Atonal Music which has no key center; literally, "absence of tonality."

Augmentation The lengthening of note values.

Band Filter A device or material used for eliminating certain chosen frequencies in order to alter tone color.

Bassoon A woodwind instrument which serves both as a melody instrument and as support for the bass in an orchestra or ensemble. Its tone is mellow and deep in the lower register, plaintive and rather piercing in the higher register. Contrabassoon (double bassoon)—the lowest member of the woodwind family, used almost exclusively as a bass instrument.

Canon A form of imitation in which each part plays or sings the same melody, entering at fixed intervals of time and pitch.

Carboys Large cylindrical containers for liquids.

Celesta A keyboard percussion instrument in which the sound is produced by hammers which strike plates of steel. Its tone is extremely pure and bell-like.

Cello (See Violoncello)

Chorale A hymn tune, usually harmonized in simple chordal style suitable for congregational singing.

Choreography An arrangement of dance movements.

Clarinet A woodwind instrument used extensively in many types of instrumental ensembles. Its tone is very bright in the upper register, mellow and rich in the lower register. Clarinets are made in a variety of sizes; the most commonly used are the clarinet in B♭, clarinet in A, bass clarinet (the lowest of the family), and the shrill E♭ clarinet, which is used primarily for special effects.

Clavichord A small keyboard instrument in which the tone is produced by metal wedges (tangents) which strike the strings as the keys are depressed. Its tone is very soft, delicate, and tender.

Coda A concluding section which is added to the main structure of a composition.

Concerto A composition for solo instrument(s) and orchestra.

Continuo The bass part which served as accompaniment in Baroque ensemble music. Usually only the bass line itself was notated; the harmonies were indicated by symbols and numbers written below the bass line. The keyboard performer would then fill in the harmonic structure and ornamentation according to these indications. Often a bass instrument such as the cello or bassoon would double the bass line.

Contralto (alto) The lowest in range of women's voices; characterized by expressive tone color.

Cornet A brass instrument similar to the trumpet, with less brilliance of tone but more agility.

Countermelody A melody added to another to provide contrast or harmonic color.

Counterpoint (contrapuntal) Music in which the chief interest lies in the satisfactory combination of various melodic strands.

Diminution The shortening of note values.

Double Bass The lowest string instrument. Its general function in the orchestra is to support the bass line; it is rarely used as a solo instrument.

Dynamics Gradations of sound intensity and volume.

Embellishments Ornamental notes which decorate a melody.

English Horn An alto woodwind instrument similar to an oboe. Its tone is expressive but dark, nasal, and highly individual.

Episode A portion of a composition which serves to provide contrast, connecting material, or modulation between the structurally significant thematic events.

Fantasia (fantasy) (free) An instrumental composition which takes its form directly from the composer's imagination rather than fixed rules.

Flute A soprano woodwind instrument with a brilliant "silvery" tone color. It is often given florid solo passages, but it is capable of an expressive lyric quality as well.

French Horn A brass instrument with a mellow, rich tone which blends so well with both woodwind and brass instruments that it is included in both woodwind and brass quintets. Its expressive tone quality makes it an important solo instrument, and it also functions effectively in subordinate roles.

Fugue A contrapuntal style of composition based on the development of a short melody, or subject, which is stated at the beginning by a single voice and imitated by other voices in close succession.

Gargoyle A grotesquely carved human or animal figure, often used as ornamentation on buildings or furniture.

Glissando A rapid slide over the scale on a keyboard instrument or harp; also, a "smeared" slur of no definite pitch intervals, possible on string instruments and trombone.

Gong A percussion instrument consisting of a broad disk of metal which is suspended from a frame and struck with a heavy drum beater.

Guiro A primitive percussion instrument consisting of a rough-sided gourd over which a stick is rubbed.

Harp A large string instrument which is plucked rather than bowed. It is capable of playing brilliant arpeggio and glissando figures with relative ease.

Harpsichord A keyboard instrument similar in shape to a small grand piano; its tones are produced by thin pieces of crow quills or leather which pluck the strings as the keys are depressed. Its clear and rather dry tone makes it particularly appropriate for performance of the contrapuntal compositions and ensemble music of the Baroque era.

Hyperprism A mathematical term representing a prism with infinite dimensions.

Improvisation The art of performing music spontaneously, without the aid of manuscript or memory.

Invention A short composition in two- or three-part counterpoint, generally for keyboard instruments.

Inversion The turning of a melody upside down so that its contour is reversed (like a mirror image).

Madrigal A type of secular choral composition that originated in Italy in the fourteenth century and was developed in the sixteenth and early seventeenth centuries into a form characterized by skillful use of contrapuntal devices.

Manual A keyboard for the hands on an organ or harpsichord.

Marimba A type of xylophone which has metal tubular resonators longer than those of a xylophone and also a softer tone quality.

Mixers Devices which make it possible to record over something that has already been recorded (overdubbing).

Motive (motif) The smallest identifiable rhythmic, melodic, or harmonic unit of a musical theme.

Oboe A soprano woodwind instrument with a penetrating, reedy quality. Its rather haunting color makes it effective in solos, especially in melancholy, sustained passages; it is also useful in adding tone color to other instruments in an ensemble or orchestra.

Oboe d'amore An eighteenth-century oboe having a pear-shaped bell similar to that of the English horn.

Ornament A standard pattern of melodic embellishment (such as trill, etc.).

Oscillator A frequency generator.

Pentatonic A five-tone scale with no half steps between any two tones, which occurs when five black keys on the piano are sounded.

Piccolo The highest member of the woodwind family, which has an extremely penetrating and bright tone.

Polyphony Music in which two or more independent voices sound simultaneously, each maintaining its own distinctive melodic line.

Polyrhythm The use of two or more contrasting rhythms played simultaneously.

Polytonality The simultaneous use of two or more melodies in different keys.

Quarter-tone An interval equal in size to one half of a semi-tone (half step).

Recorder An early type of fipple flute which has a soft and slightly reedy tone quality.

Reverberation The act of sound continuation as if in a series of echoes.

Rhapsody A very free instrumental form which is emotional and intense.

Ring Modulator A device which varies the tone quality.

Rondo A form in which the same refrain alternates between contrasting sections (A, B, A, C, A, etc.).

Scherzo In symphonies, a movement (often the third) in rapid $\frac{3}{4}$ meter, usually of a humorous nature.

Sequencer A device that is used to produce a preset voltage sequence for the purpose of controlling a series of events.

Sitar An Indian string instrument that has a long neck and a varying number of strings and is plucked.

Soprano The highest female singing voice.

Subject In fugal writing, a theme which is heard alone at the beginning of a fugue, and then is imitated by various voices.

Syncopation A shifting of the regular accents in a measure to the weaker beats.

Synthesizer An elaborate electronic instrument used for musical composition.

Tablature A system of instrumental notation indicating string, fret, key, or finger to be used instead of the pitch to be sounded.

Temple Blocks A series of hollow, circular blocks played with felt or wooden sticks.

Tenor The highest adult male singing voice.

Texture The consistency of the "musical fabric" of a composition, such as dense, airy, etc.

Timbre The quality or "color" of a tone, as is evident when the same pitch is played on various instruments or sung by various voices.

Timpani Large hemispherical drums tuned in definite pitches, used extensively in orchestral writing to underscore rhythmic figures and reinforce dynamic gradations; solo passages are also possible.

Transcribe To transfer from one performing medium to another, such as a piano transcription of an orchestral composition.

Trombone A brass instrument with a warm, solemn, and deep tone. It is well suited to prominent, heroic passages and also serves as background support.

Vibrato A slightly tremulous effect given to a tone by rapid and minute variations in pitch; executed in string instruments by a rapid movement of the left hand.

Viola The alto instrument of the string family; its tone is warm and expressive but somewhat veiled. Although it is used most frequently to play accompaniment figures or to support the harmony, solo passages are also fairly common.

Violin The soprano instrument of the string family. It is an extremely versatile instrument.

Violoncello (cello) The bass instrument of the string quartet; it is often used to provide a foundation for the string choir, but is extremely expressive as a melodic instrument as well.

Xylophone A pitched percussion instrument which can perform melodic and scale figures, glissandos, and chords; its sound is hard and dry.

Alphabetical Index of Music and Poetry

A la capotín, 152
Alegria del Alosno, 93
All Lands and Peoples, 205
Aquarius/Let the Sun Shine In, 188

Bergwalzer, Der, 156
Boléro (Ravel), 104
Bwana, Ibariki Afrika, 139

Canzona (Frescobaldi), 28
Carmina Burana (Orff), 158
Christmas Happening, A, 211
Circus Band, The, 134

Cloud-Chamber Music (Partch), 23
Come, Quiet Hour, 90
Competition and Galop (Bernstein), 85

Dance of the Comedians (Smetana), 178
Day-Glo-Day, 38
Dhun, 145
Doudlebska Polka, 181
Dripsody (Le Caine), 171

Earthwords (Hartford), 53
Ebony Concerto (Stravinsky), 85

Echigoshi, 145
Einundzwanzig, 91
Eleanor Rigby, 42
Entertaining of a Shy Little Girl, The, 200

Fantasia (Mudarra), 29
Fog (Sandburg), 167
For Us a Child Is Born, 210
Fourth of July (Ives), 130

Gargoyles (Luening), 25
Gaucho Serenade (Bolognini), 101
Get Thy Bearings, 19

Go Down Moses, 72
God's Goin' to Set This World on Fire, 74
(Good Old Electric) Washing Machine (Circa 1943), 51
Green Fields, 203
Green Green Grass of Home, 48
Guantanamera, 154
Gymnopédie No. 1 (Satie), 57

Henry Martin, 150
Heroic Music (Telemann), 97
He's Gone Away, 121
Hey, Ho! Anybody Home? 170
Hunter, The (Nash), 167
Hurdy Gurdy Man, 198
Hyperprism (Varèse), 24

I'm Gonna Be A Country Girl Again, 121
Infernal Dance of King Kastchei (Stravinsky), 179
It's About That Time (Davis), 84
It's a New Day, 16
It's a Small World, 18
I Wish I Knew How It Would Feel to Be Free, 80

Jenifer Juniper, 195
Joy Is Like the Rain, 125

Ketjak Chorus, 145
Kleine Kammermusik, Opus 24, No. 2 (Hindemith), 99

Landlord, 144
Let the Rafters Ring, 4

Madrugada, La, 151
Melody and Harmony, 90
Memories, 132
Mounsier's Almaine (Batchelar), 92

Navarraise (Massenet), 178

Nisiōtikōs Choros, 143

Of Wood and Brass (Ussachevsky), 171
O God, Our Help in Ages Past, 208
O Happy Day, 77

pai niao chao fêng, 26
Pantheistic Study for Guitar and Large Bird (Stuart), 93
Pastures of Plenty, 120
Power and Glory, The, 126
Prelude No. 2 in E Major (Villa-Lobos), 93
Revolutionary Ideas, Part I, 217
Rhapsody in Blue (Gershwin), 84
Rondo (Cowell), 169
Rondo for Bassoon and Orchestra (Weber), 169

Sarakatsani Song, 141
Scarborough Fair, 146
Scherzo (Humor) (Still), 76
Seven Variations on God Save the King (Beethoven), 58
Shalom, 161
Shalom, Chaverim, 91
Sinfonia (Berio), 31
Sing Out! 1
Sketch for Percussion (Lo Presti), 103
Soldier's Song (Kodály), 29
Sonata No. 31 in G Major (Cimarosa), 27
Sonata Number Four for Violin (Ives), 131

Son del viento, El, 152
Spinning Wheel, 35
Starlight Dance, 142
String Quartet in C Major, Opus 76, No. 3 (Haydn), 101
Summer Song, 206
Surfing Song, 207
Swingin' Round, 170
Symphony for Band, Opus 69 (Persichetti), 95
Symphony in B Flat for Concert Band (Hindemith), 88
Symphony No. 4 in F Minor, Opus 36 (Tchaikovsky), 106

Tallis' Canon, 89
This Is the Word, 31
Tree of Peace, The, 11
Two-Part Invention in D Minor (Bach), 30, 87
Two Variations on the Theme (Blood, Sweat and Tears), 57

Up and Get Us Gone, 192

Variations on "America" (Ives), 56
Violin Concerto in E Minor, Opus 64 (Mendelssohn), 28

Wade in the Water, 66
Wanderin', 115
Wayfarin' Stranger, 110
We'll Find America, 7
What a wonderful day! (Shiki), 167
What's New Pussycat? 164
When I'm Sixty-Four, 44
When the Bells Justle (Foss), 24
Whoopee Ti-Yi-Yo, 122
Who Will Buy? 160
Wreck of the Old 97, The, 50